Delightful Desserts

The Secrets to Achieving
Incredible Flavor
in Your Sweet Treats

Jane Soudah

Pastry Chef at Eveleigh, Owner of Sweet Jane's Bakeshop
and Winner of Food Network's *Spring Baking Championship*

PAGE STREET
PUBLISHING CO.

PAGE STREET
PUBLISHING CO.

First published in 2017 by
Page Street Publishing Co.
27 Congress Street, Suite 105
Salem, MA 01970
www.pagestreetpublishing.com

Distributed by Macmillan, sales in Canada by The Canadian Manda Group.

21 20 19 18 17   1 2 3 4 5

ISBN-13: 978-1-62414-423-3
ISBN-10: 1-62414-423-3

Library of Congress Control Number: 2016963581

Cover and book design by Page Street Publishing Co.
Photography by Allie Lehman

Printed and bound in China

As a member of 1% for the Planet, Page Street Publishing protects our planet by donating to nonprofits like The Trustees, which focuses on local land conservation. Learn more at onepercentfortheplanet.org.

DEDICATION

For Jemma, Madeleine, Gavin and Nicky, my gang of crazies,
for inspiring me, loving me and calling me Mom.
You are my greatest pride and loves.

CONTENTS

INTRODUCTION

I have had a love of baking for my entire life: I would arrive home from elementary school, walk in the door and ask my mom if I could make chocolate chip cookies. Every year I demanded to make my own birthday cake, and I started selling cookies, cakes and cheesecakes to friends and neighbors when I was in fifth grade. Baking is my time to create, be artistic and find my peace. It's an expression of who I am, and it allows me to share that with my friends and family.

For so many people, desserts are something sweet to end a meal. For me, they are an extension of the meal, bringing together different flavors and textures to create unique, bold desserts. These creations are not just something sweet; they are also a balance of tart, bitter, sour and salty ingredients that make a memorable ending (or beginning) to a day.

The recipes in this book have straightforward directions that are easy for novice to expert bakers to follow. They also demystify some of the more complicated pastries.

My hope is that you will take the flavors and ingredients presented in each chapter and continue to experiment with them. Find alternative citrus fruit to use in the citrus chapter (page 9) and experiment with different floral flavors (page 53). Discover uncommon bitters (page 31) or vinegars (page 107) that you think would go well in one of the recipes in this book. Use the unusual and bold flavors introduced here as a starting point to create your own daring desserts!!

Jane Sundahl

CHAPTER ONE

Citrus

I love tart desserts! As a child, I would eat an entire lemon, relishing the experience of my entire face puckering. I will ALWAYS choose a lemon dessert over anything else on a dessert menu, but I am often disappointed that there isn't enough tart-sweetness and citrus flavor. This chapter remedies that problem, and it demonstrates how to create bold lemon, grapefruit and lime desserts by combining and layering citrus and tart ingredients.

LEMON BARS

These lemon bars are a lemon-lover's dream! There is lemon zest flecked throughout the shortbread crust, and a variety of lemon ingredients in the custard add deep citrus flavor and tartness. The result is an addictive, sweet-sour lemon bar.

YIELD: 16 BARS

2 cups (250 g) all-purpose flour

½ cup plus ¼ cup (98 g) powdered sugar, divided

1 tbsp (10 g) lemon zest

1 cup (230 g) cold butter, cubed

FILLING

4 large eggs

2 cups (384 g) sugar

1 tbsp (7 g) lemon juice powder

2 tbsp (20 g) lemon zest

¼ cup (60 ml) fresh lemon juice

¼ cup (60 ml) bottled lemon juice

½ tsp lemon oil

½ tsp citric acid

½ tsp baking powder

¼ cup (31 g) all-purpose flour

Preheat the oven to 350°F (177°C, or gas mark 4). Line a 9 x 13 x 2-inch (23 x 33 x 5-cm) baking pan with parchment paper or nonstick foil.

In the bowl of a stand mixer fitted with the paddle attachment, combine the flour, ½ cup (65 g) of powdered sugar and the lemon zest. Add the cold butter and mix on medium-low speed until the mixture resembles sand. Press the mixture into the prepared pan. Bake for 20 to 25 minutes until the edges are light golden brown.

While the crust bakes, in the bowl of a stand mixer fitted with the whisk attachment, whisk together the eggs, sugar, lemon juice powder, lemon zest, lemon juices, lemon oil and citric acid until smooth. Add the baking powder and flour, and mix well.

Pour the filling mixture over the baked and still-warm crust. Bake for an additional 20 to 25 minutes until the filling is set. Let cool for 30 minutes. Sprinkle with ¼ cup (33 g) of powdered sugar and cut into squares.

LEMON-GLAZED MADELEINES

I have a weakness for small French pastries that can be enjoyed with a cup of coffee for breakfast, particularly the madeleine, which is an all-time favorite. My affection for this pastry even extended to my daughter, whose name is spelled exactly like this delectable French cake. Plan ahead when making this dessert as the batter needs to be refrigerated for at least one hour, but preferably overnight. A longer rest in the refrigerator results in a better texture and the much-desired characteristic madeleine "hump." You will need madeleine pans to make these pastries.

YIELD: 18 CAKES

½ cup plus 2 tbsp (145 g) butter, divided
⅔ cup (127 g) sugar
2 large eggs
¼ tsp lemon oil
½ tsp lemon juice powder
1 tbsp (10 g) fresh lemon zest
3 tbsp (45 ml) whole milk
1 cup (125 g) all-purpose flour
1 tsp baking powder
¼ tsp kosher salt

LEMON GLAZE
1 cup (130 g) powdered sugar, sifted
4 tbsp (60 ml) fresh lemon juice

Melt ½ cup (115 g) of butter in a small saucepan. Set aside to cool to room temperature.

In a large bowl, combine the sugar and eggs. Using a hand mixer, whisk together until light and slightly thickened, approximately 2 minutes. Mix in the lemon oil, lemon juice powder, lemon zest and milk. Add the flour, baking powder and salt, whisking until just combined. Add the melted butter and fold into the batter using a rubber spatula. Cover the bowl with plastic wrap, and refrigerate for a minimum of 1 hour to overnight.

Preheat the oven to 400°F (204°C, or gas mark 6). Melt the remaining 2 tablespoons (30 g) of butter.

Brush the madeleine pans generously with butter and place in the freezer for the butter to harden. Fill each indentation in the pan ¾ full. Bake for 12 to 15 minutes until the cakes are golden brown. Allow to cool in the pans for 5 minutes before removing.

Whisk together the powdered sugar and lemon juice in a small bowl until smooth.

While the cakes are still warm, dip each cake into the glaze. Place the glazed cakes on a cooling rack that has been placed over a baking sheet, allowing the glaze to harden and the cakes to cool completely.

PALOMA CAKE

I am lucky to live in Southern California where citrus trees grow in abundance, including in my own backyard. With two heavily-laden grapefruit trees in my garden, I am always trying to find ways to use the plethora of fruit. One of my favorite summer cocktails is a Paloma, a refreshing combination of grapefruit juice, grapefruit soda and tequila. This cake is an ode to that drink. It's a fabulous use for grapefruit, and it's especially delicious when paired with its namesake.

YIELD: 12 TO 16 SERVINGS

1 lb (454 g) ruby red grapefruit, approximately 2 large fruit

1 cup (230 g) butter, room temperature

1¼ cups (240 g) sugar

3 large eggs

2½ cups (312 g) all-purpose flour

¼ tsp kosher salt

¼ tsp baking soda

½ tsp baking powder

GLAZE

2 tbsp (30 ml) fresh grapefruit juice

1 tbsp (15 ml) tequila

1 cup (130 g) powdered sugar, sifted

Pinch of kosher salt

Preheat the oven to 325°F (163°C, or gas mark 3). Grease an 8-cup (1-kg) Bundt pan with nonstick cooking spray.

Wash and scrub the grapefruit. Dry the grapefruit and zest them to get 1 tablespoon (10 g) of zest. Peel the grapefruit and purée the entire fruit in a blender or with an immersion blender, then measure 1½ cups (370 g) of grapefruit purée for the cake.

In the bowl of a stand mixer fitted with the paddle attachment, cream together the butter and sugar until light and fluffy, approximately 2 minutes. Add the eggs, one at a time, mixing well after each addition. Mix in the grapefruit zest and purée. Add the flour, salt, baking soda and baking powder. Mix until well combined, scraping the sides and bottom of the bowl with a rubber spatula.

Pour the batter into the prepared pan. Bake for 45 to 50 minutes until the cake is golden brown and a cake tester inserted into the middle of the cake comes out clean.

While the cake is baking, whisk together the grapefruit juice, tequila, powdered sugar and salt until smooth.

Cool the cake in the pan for 20 minutes before removing from the pan and cooling completely on a wire rack. Place the cooled cake on its wire rack over a baking sheet. Pour the glaze over the top of the cake, allowing it to drizzle down the sides.

LIME DRIZZLE CAKE

This simple, yet impressive cake comes together quickly, and it has layers of fresh lime flavor and zestiness. My sons often beg me to make this cake for them and even offer to pick fresh limes from our tree to aid in their request. You can substitute lemon juice and zest for the lime ingredients in this recipe for a fabulous lemon drizzle cake as well.

YIELD: 8 TO 10 SERVINGS

1½ cups (187 g) all-purpose flour

½ tsp kosher salt

½ tsp baking powder

¾ cup (172 g) butter, room temperature

4 oz (113 g) cream cheese, room temperature

1½ cups (288 g) sugar

1 tbsp (10 g) fresh lime zest

2 tbsp (30 ml) fresh lime juice

3 large eggs

SYRUP

⅓ cup (78 ml) fresh lime juice

⅓ cup (64 g) sugar

GLAZE

¾ cup (98 g) powdered sugar, sifted

½ tsp fresh lime zest

2 tbsp (30 ml) fresh lime juice

Preheat the oven to 325°F (163°C, or gas mark 3). Grease a 9 x 5 x 3-inch (23 x 13 x 8-cm) loaf pan with nonstick cooking spray.

In a small bowl, whisk together the flour, salt and baking powder. In the bowl of a stand mixer fitted with the paddle attachment, cream together the butter, cream cheese, sugar, lime zest and lime juice until light and fluffy, approximately 2 minutes.

Add the eggs, one at a time, mixing well after each addition and scraping the sides and bottom of bowl with a rubber spatula. Add the flour mixture, mixing until just combined. Pour the batter into the prepared pan. Bake for 70 to 75 minutes until the cake is golden brown and a cake tester inserted into the middle of the cake comes out clean.

While the cake is baking, combine the lime juice and sugar in a small saucepan. Bring to a boil over medium heat, stirring to dissolve the sugar. Once the sugar is dissolved, remove from the heat and cool to room temperature.

Whisk together the powdered sugar, lime zest and lime juice until smooth.

While the cake is still hot, pour the lime syrup over the top of the cake. Cool the cake in the pan for 20 minutes, allowing the syrup to soak into the cake. Remove the cake from the pan, place on a wire rack and cool completely. Once the cake is cooled, pour the glaze over the top of the loaf, letting the glaze drizzle down the sides.

LEMON CURD

As a child growing up in England, I attended a fair number of afternoon high teas where I was introduced to lemon curd, which began a lifelong love affair. It would be spread on scones and paired with Devonshire cream, the tangy lemon complementing the rich, thick cream. I often make a double batch of this lemon curd to keep in my fridge. I use it in many of the recipes in this chapter as well as spreading it on toast or scones. You can substitute any citrus fruit for the lemon in this recipe to make different flavored curds. Save the egg whites to make the Lemon Pavlova with Blueberry-Thyme Compote (page 29).

YIELD: APPROXIMATELY 1½ CUPS (181 G)

½ cup (115 g) butter
¾ cup (144 g) sugar
½ cup (118 ml) fresh lemon juice
¼ cup (40 g) grated lemon zest
Pinch of kosher salt
8 egg yolks, room temperature

In a medium saucepan, melt the butter. Add the sugar, lemon juice, lemon zest, salt and egg yolks, and whisk until combined. Cook over medium-low heat, stirring constantly, until the mixture is thickened (5 to 7 minutes) and the temperature on an instant-read thermometer reads 175°F (80°C).

Remove from the heat and pour the hot lemon curd through a fine-mesh sieve into a clean container. While the lemon curd is still warm, blend with an immersion blender until the lemon curd is creamy, approximately 1 minute. Cover the lemon curd with plastic wrap and refrigerate until cold, 2 to 3 hours.

LEMON CURD CHEESECAKE

The addition of lemon curd to this lemon-scented cheesecake adds a burst of tart, lemony flavor to the creamy richness of the cheesecake batter. Lemon sandwich cookies are used for the crust as they add another layer of lemon flavor to this cheesecake.

YIELD: 12 TO 16 SERVINGS

1½ cups (135 g) lemon sandwich-cookie crumbs, approximately 20 cookies

2 lb (907 g) full-fat cream cheese, room temperature

1½ cups (288 g) sugar

¼ tsp kosher salt

5 large eggs

1 cup (230 g) sour cream, room temperature

½ cup (118 ml) lemon juice

2 tsp (7 g) fresh lemon zest

⅔ cup (80 g) Lemon Curd (page 18)

Preheat the oven to 350°F (177°C, or gas mark 4). Wrap the outside of a 9-inch (23-cm) round springform pan with a double thickness of aluminum foil, making sure there are no holes in the foil.

Pat the cookie crumbs into the bottom of the springform pan. Bake for 12 to 15 minutes. Cool completely while making the cheesecake filling. Reduce the oven to 325°F (163°C, or gas mark 3).

Place the cream cheese, sugar and salt in the bowl of a food processor, and mix until well blended. Add the eggs and process until smooth. Add the sour cream, lemon juice and lemon zest, and pulse until completely combined and smooth. Pour the filling into the crust.

Dollop spoonfuls of lemon curd over the top of the cheesecake filling and swirl with a knife. Place the springform pan into a large roasting pan and pour enough hot water into the roasting pan to come halfway up the sides of the springform pan.

Bake for 1 hour and 10 minutes until the cheesecake is just set in the center. Turn the oven off, keep the door closed and let the cheesecake stand in the oven for 1 hour. Remove the cheesecake from the water bath and cool completely to room temperature. Refrigerate for 6 hours to overnight.

YUZU-LIME PIE

Yuzu is a citrus fruit from Asia. Compared to other citrus, it has a floral tartness; its flavor is often described as a cross between a sour mandarin and kaffir lime. I love the floral notes it adds to my version of key lime pie. This pie is a perfect combination of creamy, sweet and tart.

YIELD: 8 TO 10 SERVINGS

1¼ cups (113 g) graham cracker crumbs
2 tbsp (24 g) sugar
5 tbsp (74 ml) butter, melted

FILLING
6 egg yolks
2 (14-oz [396-g]) cans sweetened condensed milk
½ cup (118 ml) fresh lime juice
½ cup (118 ml) bottled yuzu juice
1 tbsp (10 g) fresh lime zest
¾ cup (177 ml) heavy cream
2 tbsp (16 g) powdered sugar

Preheat the oven to 350°F (177°C, or gas mark 4).

In a medium bowl, stir together the graham cracker crumbs and sugar. Add the melted butter, and stir until the crumbs are evenly coated. Press the crumb mixture into bottom and sides of a 9-inch (23-cm) deep-dish pie pan. Bake for 10 minutes. While the crust is baking, prepare the filling.

In a medium bowl, whisk together the egg yolks. Add the sweetened condensed milk, lime juice, yuzu juice and lime zest. Whisk until combined and smooth.

Pour the filling into the baked crust, and bake for 15 minutes until the center is just set. Cool completely to room temperature, and then refrigerate for at least 4 hours.

In the bowl of a stand mixer fitted with the whisk attachment, combine the heavy cream and powdered sugar. Whisk until soft peaks form. Top each serving of pie with a dollop of whipped cream.

LEMON BUTTER CAKE

This cake is loaded with lemon flavor. It uses lemon oil, zest and lemon juice powder, and it is soaked with a lemon juice–butter glaze. It is truly a one-bowl cake where you put all the cake ingredients in the mixer bowl at once and mix together. I like to call this an "all-day cake" because it's fabulous for breakfast, late-morning snack, afternoon tea and evening dessert!

YIELD: 12 TO 16 SERVINGS

1 cup (230 g) butter, room temperature

2 cups (384 g) sugar

4 large eggs

1 tbsp (10 g) lemon zest

1 tsp lemon oil

1 tbsp (12 g) lemon juice powder

3 cups (375 g) all-purpose flour

1 tsp kosher salt

1 tsp baking powder

½ tsp baking soda

1 cup (237 ml) buttermilk, room temperature

GLAZE

½ cup (115 g) butter

1¼ cups (240 g) sugar

6 tbsp (88 ml) lemon juice

Pinch of kosher salt

Preheat the oven to 325°F (163°C, or gas mark 3). Grease an 8-cup (1-kg) Bundt pan with nonstick spray.

In the bowl of a stand mixer fitted with the paddle attachment, place the butter, sugar, eggs, lemon zest, lemon oil, lemon juice powder, flour, salt, baking powder, baking soda and buttermilk. Mix on low speed for 1 minute. Increase the speed to medium and mix for an additional 4 minutes.

Pour the batter into the prepared pan. Bake for 50 minutes, until a cake tester inserted into the center of the cake comes out clean.

While the cake is baking, combine the butter, sugar, lemon juice and salt in a small saucepan for the glaze. Cook over medium heat until the butter is melted and the sugar is dissolved, about 5 minutes. Do not boil the glaze. Cool to room temperature.

While the cake is still warm, poke holes all over it with a metal or wooden skewer. Slowly pour the glaze in 3 increments over the cake in the pan, allowing the glaze to soak into the cake before adding more glaze. Cool the cake completely in the pan before removing.

GRAPEFRUIT TART

Every winter, I buy cases of ruby red grapefruit from my children's school fundraiser, and we end up eating and drinking them at almost every meal. With such an ample supply of grapefruit, I was inspired to create a tart based on the classic French lemon tart. A tangy, silky grapefruit custard is baked into a butter cookie (sablé) crust and finished with a light dusting of powdered sugar. The sablé crust recipe makes enough dough for two tarts. Feel free to use half the dough for this tart and use the other half to make the Salted Caramel Chocolate Tart (page 144).

YIELD: 8 SERVINGS

½ cup plus 1 tbsp (130 g) butter, room temperature

½ cup (96 g) sugar

¼ tsp kosher salt

1 large egg

1¾ cups (219 g) all-purpose flour

FILLING

4 large eggs

⅓ cup (78 ml) heavy cream

¾ cup (144 g) sugar

½ cup plus 2 tbsp (148 ml) fresh ruby red grapefruit juice

2 tsp (7 g) ruby red grapefruit zest

Pinch of kosher salt

2 tbsp (16 g) powdered sugar

Preheat the oven to 350°F (177°C, or gas mark 4).

Cream together the butter, sugar and salt in the bowl of a stand mixer fitted with the paddle attachment. Add the egg and mix until blended. Add the flour and mix on low speed until just incorporated.

Divide the dough into 2 discs. Wrap 1 portion of dough in plastic wrap and save for future use. The dough can be refrigerated for up to a week or kept frozen for up to 1 month.

Roll the second portion of dough out on a lightly floured surface to an 11-inch (28-cm) round and gently fit into a 9-inch (23-cm) tart pan with removable bottom, pressing into the sides of the tart pan. Trim the edges of the crust even with the top of the pan.

Refrigerate the tart shell for 30 minutes. Prick the bottom of the tart shell with the tines of a fork. Bake for 15 to 20 minutes until the entire shell is a light golden brown.

Reduce the oven temperature to 325°F (163°C, or gas mark 3) and place the cooked tart shell on a parchment-lined baking sheet.

Whisk together the eggs, heavy cream, sugar, grapefruit juice, grapefruit zest and salt in a medium bowl until completely combined. Pour into the tart shell, and bake for 25 minutes until the filling has set. The center of the tart should have a very slight jiggle. Cool completely to room temperature. Place the powdered sugar in a small, fine-mesh sieve and sprinkle over the top of the cooled tart.

LEMON PAVLOVA WITH BLUEBERRY-THYME COMPOTE

Pavlovas are a cloud of meringue with a crunchy exterior and a chewy, marshmallow-like center and topped with whipped cream and fresh fruit. This pavlova uses both whipped cream and Lemon Curd (page 18) and is topped with the Blueberry-Thyme Compote (page 74). When in season, fresh berries, such as raspberries, strawberries, blueberries and blackberries, would also be a nice addition. When whipping the egg whites for the meringue, use a very clean bowl to ensure that the egg whites get the most volume.

YIELD: 6 TO 8 SERVINGS

1 cup (192 g) sugar

1 tbsp (9 g) cornstarch

3 large egg whites, room temperature

Pinch of kosher salt

3 tbsp (45 ml) cold water

1 tsp white vinegar

1 cup (240 ml) heavy cream

1 tbsp (8 g) powdered sugar

⅔ cup (80 g) Lemon Curd (page 18)

1 cup (246 g) Blueberry-Thyme Compote (page 74)

Preheat the oven to 300°F (149°C, or gas mark 2). Draw an 8-inch (20-cm) circle with pencil on a piece of parchment paper, turn it over and place it on a baking sheet.

Whisk together the sugar and cornstarch in a small bowl. In the bowl of a stand mixer fitted with the whisk attachment, whisk together the egg whites and salt on high until soft peaks form, 5 to 7 minutes. Add the water; the mixture may deflate a little bit. Beat again until soft peaks form, 5 minutes. Reduce the mixer speed to low and add the sugar-cornstarch mixture, 1 tablespoon (9 g) at a time, beating to incorporate after each addition. Add the vinegar and increase the mixer to high speed. Mix until glossy and stiff peaks form, approximately 5 minutes.

Mound the meringue on the parchment paper within the circle. Using a spoon, make a 5-inch (13-cm) round indentation in the center of the mound. Bake for 40 to 45 minutes until the meringue is a light golden brown and crisp on the outside. Turn the oven off, prop the door open and allow the meringue to cool in the oven for 1 hour.

When ready to serve the pavlova, combine heavy cream and powdered sugar in the bowl of a stand mixer fitted with the whisk attachment. Beat at medium-high until soft peaks form, 4 to 6 minutes. Fill the center of meringue with the whipped cream, top with lemon curd, then spoon blueberry compote over the lemon curd, allowing it to drizzle down the sides of the meringue. Serve immediately.

CHAPTER TWO

Bitters

My favorite cocktail is an old-fashioned made with whiskey, sugar, orange zest and aromatic bitters. The first time I had an old-fashioned I was amazed at how the bitters—a tincture of various herbs, barks, roots and plants—transformed a glass of whiskey. This chapter explores the addition of aromatic and flavored bitters to create bold desserts with the bitter notes accenting and elevating the flavors to a whole new level. A few of the desserts in this chapter are based on some of my favorite cocktails.

JANE'S OLD-FASHIONED

A chapter on the use of bitters in desserts would not be complete without the original source that started my love of bitters. This is my take on the classic cocktail, and it is still my favorite drink. Friends always request a "Jane's Old-Fashioned" when they are at my house. I use good cocktail cherries as a garnish, so definitely splurge on a jar. Their flavor really adds a boost to this delicious cocktail.

YIELD: 1 DRINK

½ cup (96 g) sugar

½ cup (120 ml) water

Peel from 1 orange removed using a vegetable peeler

OLD-FASHIONED

3 fluid oz (90 ml) rye whiskey (I like to use either Buffalo Trace or Bulleit.)

1 tbsp (15 ml) orange simple syrup

4 dashes angostura bitters

1 Luxardo or amarena cherry with its syrup

1½-inch (4-cm) strip of orange peel, removed using a vegetable peeler

1 large ice cube

In a small saucepan, make the orange simple syrup by mixing together the sugar and water. Bring to a boil and cook until the sugar has dissolved, about 2 minutes. Remove from the heat and add the orange peel. Allow the syrup to steep for 30 minutes. Remove the peel. Orange simple syrup can be stored in the refrigerator for up to 1 month.

Combine the whiskey, orange simple syrup, bitters and cherry in a whiskey glass, stirring well. Squeeze the piece of orange peel over the top of the drink and rub it along the rim of the glass. Add the peel to the drink. Finish with a large ice cube and enjoy!

CHOCOLATE CHILI BITTERS FUDGE COOKIES

These are a brownie in cookie form! They have a crisp exterior and a fudgy center. The bitter chocolate is enhanced by the use of both chocolate chili bitters and ancho chili powder. The cookies have a slight spice and smokiness that make them sophisticated and daring. Make sure not to overbake these cookies to keep their fudgy interior.

YIELD: 18 COOKIES

3 cups (540 g) bittersweet chocolate chips, divided

6 tbsp (86 g) butter

¼ cup (31 g) all-purpose flour

¼ tsp baking powder

½ tsp kosher salt

¼ tsp ancho chili powder

2 large eggs

½ cup (96 g) granulated sugar

¼ cup (55 g) dark brown sugar, packed

2 tsp (10 ml) chocolate chili bitters

1 cup (116 g) chopped walnuts, toasted

Preheat the oven to 350°F (177°C, or gas mark 4). Line 3 baking sheets with parchment paper.

In a medium, microwave-safe bowl, melt together 1 cup (180 g) of chocolate chips and the butter, 1 minute 30 seconds to 2 minutes 30 seconds. Allow to cool to room temperature.

In a small bowl, whisk together the flour, baking powder, salt and ancho powder, and set aside. In the bowl of a stand mixer fitted with the whisk attachment, mix together the eggs, granulated sugar, brown sugar and bitters. Continue whisking on high speed until the mixture is slightly thickened and light in color, approximately 2 minutes.

Add the cooled chocolate mixture and mix on low speed until combined. Add the dry ingredients and mix on low until the flour is just incorporated, scraping down the sides and bottom of the bowl with a rubber spatula.

Remove the bowl from the mixer. Fold in the remaining 2 cups (360 g) of chocolate chips and the walnuts. Cover the bowl with plastic wrap, and refrigerate the batter for 30 minutes.

Using a 1⅓-ounce (38-g) cookie scoop (red handled) drop the batter onto the prepared baking sheets, 6 cookies per sheet as the cookies will spread during baking. Bake for 10 to 11 minutes. The edges of the cookies will be set and the tops of the cookies will still look slightly wet. Cool completely before removing from the baking sheets.

ORANGE BITTERS—OLIVE OIL CAKE WITH APEROL GLAZE

This cake is inspired by one of my favorite summer cocktails—the Aperol Spritz. I've re-created the flavors of the cocktail using fresh orange zest, orange juice, orange bitters and Aperol. Use a light citrusy olive oil in this cake. One of my favorite things about making this cake is being able to walk out my kitchen door and pick fresh oranges from the trees in my backyard. Oranges from your local grocery store will work just as well.

YIELD: 12 SERVINGS

1¼ cups (296 ml) whole milk

½ cup (118 ml) fresh orange juice

2 tsp (10 ml) orange bitters

1 tbsp (10 g) orange zest

2 cups (250 g) all-purpose flour

1 tsp kosher salt

½ tsp baking powder

½ tsp baking soda

3 large eggs

2 cups (384 g) granulated sugar

1 cup (237 ml) extra-virgin olive oil

APEROL GLAZE

1½ cups (195 g) powdered sugar

1 tbsp (15 ml) Aperol

3 tbsp (45 ml) orange juice

1 tsp orange zest

¼ tsp orange bitters

Preheat the oven to 350°F (177°C, or gas mark 4). Grease an 8-cup (1-kg) Bundt pan with nonstick cooking spray.

In a small bowl, combine the milk, orange juice, orange bitters and orange zest. The mixture might start to curdle, which is fine. In another bowl, whisk together the flour, salt, baking powder and baking soda. In the bowl of an electric mixer fitted with the whisk attachment, combine the eggs and granulated sugar, and whisk them together.

With the mixer on low speed, slowly stream in the olive oil 1 tablespoon (15 ml) at a time. Whisk well after each addition. Do not add the next tablespoon (15 ml) of olive oil until the previous one is completely combined. Continue whisking until all of the oil is emulsified into the sugar-egg mixture.

Add the wet ingredients in 3 additions, alternating with the dry ingredients in 2 additions, starting and ending with the wet ingredients. Mix well after each addition.

Pour the batter into the prepared cake pan. Bake for 45 to 55 minutes until the cake is deep golden brown and a cake tester inserted into the middle of the cake comes out clean.

While the cake is baking, whisk together the powdered sugar, Aperol, orange juice, orange zest and orange bitters until smooth.

Cool the cake in the pan for 20 minutes before removing from the pan and cooling completely on a wire rack. Place the cooled cake on its wire rack over a baking sheet. Pour glaze over the top of the cake, allowing it to drizzle down the sides.

ARABIC COFFEE AND CARDAMOM BITTERS CRÈME BRÛLÉE

This dessert is an ode to my Palestinian heritage. Whenever we would visit my paternal grandparents, who immigrated to the United States from Jerusalem, Arabic coffee would be offered. I fondly remember the air perfumed with the aroma of coffee and cardamom while my grandparents pinched my cheeks and exclaimed how much I'd grown. This crème brûlée is an ode to that memory. The creamy coffee custard is scented with cardamom bitters, and the caramelized sugar topping accents the bitter coffee.

YIELD: 6 CRÈME BRÛLÉES

2 cups (437 ml) heavy cream
¾ cup (144 g) sugar
1 tbsp (3 g) instant espresso powder
Pinch of kosher salt
2½ tsp (12 ml) cardamom bitters
5 egg yolks, room temperature
9 tbsp (108 g) superfine sugar

Preheat the oven to 300°F (149°C, or gas mark 2). Arrange 6 crème brûlée dishes or ramekins in two 9 x 13 x 2-inch (23 x 33 x 5-cm) baking pans or a large roasting pan.

In a medium saucepan, combine the heavy cream, sugar, espresso powder and salt. Bring to a boil over medium-high heat, stirring to dissolve the sugar and espresso powder, about 2 to 4 minutes. Remove from the heat and add the cardamom bitters.

In a medium bowl, whisk the egg yolks. Add the warm cream mixture in a slow stream to the egg yolks, whisking constantly. Strain the custard through a fine-mesh sieve into a clean bowl or liquid measuring cup.

Divide the custard between the dishes, filling each ¾ full. Carefully pour enough hot water into each baking pan to come halfway up the sides of the dishes. Cover the pans with foil. Bake for 20 minutes until the edges of the custard are set, but the center has a slight jiggle when the dish is lightly shaken.

Remove the dishes from the water bath and let cool completely to room temperature. Refrigerate for at least 2 hours. Just before serving, sprinkle the top of each custard evenly with 1½ tablespoons (18 g) of superfine sugar. Use a kitchen blowtorch to evenly melt and caramelize the sugar. Allow the caramelized sugar to cool and harden for approximately 5 minutes before serving.

BROWN SUGAR AND LAVENDER BITTERS POTS DE CRÈME

I was gifted some homemade brown sugar and lavender body scrub for my birthday a few years ago. Breathing in the scent of brown sugar and lavender essential oil inspired this new dessert combination. The lavender flavor in the brown sugar–baked custard comes from the use of lavender bitters. Top with my Lavender Caramel Sauce (page 66) and a generous dollop of fresh Whipped Cream (page 147).

YIELD: 8 POTS DE CRÈME

2 cups (237 ml) heavy cream

½ cup (110 g) dark brown sugar, packed

½ tsp kosher salt

2 tsp (10 ml) lavender bitters

6 egg yolks, room temperature

8 tbsp (200 g) Lavender Caramel Sauce (page 66), warmed

Fresh Whipped Cream (page 147)

Preheat the oven to 350°F (177°C, or gas mark 4). Arrange eight 4-ounce (113-g) mason jars in a 9 x 13 x 2-inch (23 x 33 x 5-cm) baking pan or a large roasting pan.

In a medium saucepan, combine the heavy cream, brown sugar and salt. Bring to a simmer over medium-high heat, stirring to dissolve the sugar, about 2 minutes. Remove from the heat and add the lavender bitters.

In a medium bowl, whisk the egg yolks. Add the warm cream mixture in a slow stream to the egg yolks, whisking constantly. Strain the custard through a fine-mesh sieve into a clean bowl or liquid measuring cup. Divide the custard between the jars, filling each ¾ full.

Carefully pour enough hot water into the baking pan to come halfway up the sides of the jars. Cover the pan with foil. Bake for 25 to 30 minutes until the edges of the custard are set, but the center has a slight jiggle when the dish is lightly shaken.

Remove the dishes from the water bath and let them cool completely to room temperature. Refrigerate for at least 2 hours. Just before serving, top each pot de crème with 1 tablespoon (25 g) of lavender caramel sauce and a dollop of whipped cream.

CHOCOLATE BITTERS CHEESECAKE

A very dear family friend used to make her chocolate cheesecake every time we would have dinner at her house. This is my ode to and version of that much-loved dessert. I used angostura bitters to complement the deep chocolate flavor. Feel free to play with different bitters, such as orange, lavender or coffee, in this cheesecake to create other unique flavor combinations.

YIELD: 12 TO 16 SERVINGS

1½ cups (135 g) chocolate sandwich-cookie crumbs, approximately 20 cookies

3 tbsp (43 g) butter, melted

24 oz (680 g) full-fat cream cheese, room temperature

1 cup (192 g) sugar

½ tsp kosher salt

3 large eggs, room temperature

2 egg yolks, room temperature

12 oz (340 g) bittersweet chocolate chips, melted and cooled

2 tbsp (7 g) espresso powder dissolved in 2 tbsp (30 ml) hot water

½ cup (118 ml) heavy cream

2 tsp (10 ml) angostura bitters

2 tbsp (16 g) all-purpose flour

Preheat the oven to 350°F (177°C, or gas mark 4). Wrap the outside of a 9-inch (23-cm) round springform pan with a double thickness of aluminum foil, making sure there are no holes in the foil.

In a medium bowl, mix together the cookie crumbs and melted butter. Pat the crumb mixture into the bottom of the springform pan, and bake for 12 to 15 minutes. Cool while making the cheesecake filling.

Place the cream cheese, sugar and salt in the bowl of a food processor. Mix until well blended. Add the eggs and egg yolks, and process until smooth. Add the melted chocolate, dissolved espresso powder, heavy cream, bitters and flour. Pulse until completely combined and smooth. Pour the filling into the crust.

Place the springform pan into a large roasting pan. Pour enough hot water into the roasting pan to come halfway up the sides of the springform pan. Bake for 40 to 50 minutes until the cheesecake is just set in the center. Turn the oven off, keep the door closed and let the cheesecake stand in the oven for 1 hour. Remove the cheesecake from the water bath and cool completely to room temperature. Refrigerate for 6 hours to overnight.

CHOCOLATE OLD-FASHIONED CAKE WITH BITTERS-ORANGE MARMALADE ICE CREAM

I am known to add alcohol to many of my desserts, earning me the nickname "The Boozy Baker," so it is unsurprising that this cake is based on my favorite cocktail. The combination of chocolate, angostura bitters and orange zest compliments the whiskey-bitters mixture that is poured over the cake while it is cooling. Serve with Cherry Balsamic Sauce (page 108) for a spectacular dessert.

YIELD: 8 SERVINGS

1 cup (230 g) butter

1 cup (180 g) bittersweet chocolate chips

1⅓ cups (256 g) sugar

5 large eggs

1½ tsp (8 ml) angostura bitters, divided

½ tsp kosher salt

½ tsp grated orange zest

1 tbsp (8 g) flour

¼ cup (60 ml) bourbon

BITTERS-ORANGE
MARMALADE ICE CREAM

2 cups (473 ml) heavy cream

1 cup (237 ml) whole milk

¾ cup (144 g) sugar

¼ tsp kosher salt

2 large eggs

1 tsp angostura bitters

½ cup (160 g) orange marmalade

Preheat the oven to 375°F (191°C, or gas mark 5). Line the bottom of a 9-inch (23-cm) round springform pan with parchment paper.

Melt the butter in a medium saucepan over medium-low heat, add the chocolate chips and remove from the heat. Let the chocolate sit in the warm butter for 3 to 5 minutes, and then mix the chocolate and butter together until smooth. Stir in the sugar. Add the eggs, one at a time, mixing well after each addition. Add 1 teaspoon (5 ml) of bitters, salt, orange zest and flour, mixing until just combined.

Pour the batter into the prepared pan, and bake for 20 to 25 minutes. The edges of the cake will be set, but the middle of the cake should still have a slight jiggle. While the cake is cooking, combine the bourbon and remaining ½ teaspoon (3 ml) bitters.

Cool the cake for 5 minutes. Pour the bourbon mixture over the top of the cake, allowing it to soak into the warm cake. Cool to room temperature before serving.

Combine the heavy cream, milk, sugar and salt in a medium saucepan. Heat the mixture to just below a boil. While the cream mixture is heating, whisk the eggs in a medium heatproof bowl. Add the hot cream in a steady stream to the eggs, whisking constantly.

Pour the mixture back into the saucepan and cook over medium-low heat, stirring constantly, until slightly thickened and an instant-read thermometer reads 175°F (80°C), about 5 to 7 minutes.

Pour the custard through a fine-mesh sieve into a clean bowl. Add the bitters and orange marmalade. Whisk until the marmalade has melted into the warm custard. Cool to room temperature.

Cover with plastic wrap and refrigerate until cold, at least 4 hours to overnight. Freeze in an ice cream maker according to the manufacturer's instructions.

PUMPKIN BITTERS AND CANDIED PUMPKIN FLAN

A very dear friend of mine is originally from Brazil, and he frequently lets me know that his most favorite dessert is flan, bemoaning how hard it is to find a flan that meets his particular standards. I asked him to taste this pumpkin flan after I created it for this cookbook. He took one bite and was silent; he took another and shook his head at me. The only thought I had was "he hates it," and I immediately started thinking of ways to improve it. When he finally spoke, all he said was "it's perfect."

YIELD: 8 TO 10 SERVINGS

¼ to ½ small sugar or pie pumpkin, seeded and peeled

1½ cups (288 g) sugar, divided

½ cup (118 ml) water

8 oz (227 g) full-fat cream cheese, room temperature

6 large eggs

1 (14-oz [397-g]) can sweetened condensed milk

1 cup (237 ml) heavy cream

½ cup (90 g) canned pumpkin purée

3 tsp (15 ml) pumpkin or holiday bitters

½ tsp kosher salt

½ tsp ground cinnamon

Preheat the oven to 350°F (177°C, or gas mark 4). Using a very sharp knife or a mandoline, slice the pumpkin into thin slices. You will need approximately 15 to 20 slices.

In a small saucepan, mix together 1 cup (192 g) of sugar and the water. Bring to a boil over medium-high heat and continue to cook, without stirring, until the sugar is caramelized and a deep golden brown, about 5 to 8 minutes. Immediately pour the caramel into the bottom of a 9½-inch (24-cm) deep-dish pie plate.

While the caramel is still warm, arrange the pumpkin slices in one layer on top of the caramel, slightly overlapping them. Place the remaining ½ cup (96 g) of sugar, cream cheese and eggs in the bowl of a food processor. Process until well blended. Add the sweetened condensed milk, heavy cream, pumpkin purée, bitters, salt and cinnamon. Process until smooth and well combined.

Slowly pour the filling into the pie dish over the caramel and pumpkin slices, taking care not to disturb the pumpkin. Place the pie dish into a large roasting pan, and pour enough hot water into the roasting pan to come halfway up the sides of the dish. Cover the roasting pan tightly with foil.

Bake for 40 to 45 minutes until the edges of the flan are set and the center has a slight jiggle. Remove the flan from the water bath and let cool to room temperature.

The flan can be served at room temperature, or it can be refrigerated for 4 hours to overnight and served cold. To unmold the flan, run a knife around the edges to loosen it from the pie dish and invert it onto a serving plate, pouring any remaining caramel in the dish over the top of the flan.

BOURBON-BITTERS PECAN BARS

I am not allowed to attend any Thanksgiving celebration without bringing my Bourbon Pecan Pie, but sometimes an entire pie seems like too much of a dessert commitment, so I created these cookie bars to satisfy pecan pie cravings. The floral, bitter notes of the angostura bitters complement the brown sugar, pecans and bourbon in these bars. These are delicious eaten on their own, but a scoop of Vanilla Ice Cream (page 147) or a dollop of fresh Whipped Cream (page 147) is a welcome addition!

YIELD: 24 SQUARES

1¼ cups (287 g) butter, room temperature

½ cup (96 g) granulated sugar

1 egg yolk

2½ cups (312 g) all-purpose flour

½ tsp kosher salt

FILLING

1 cup (220 g) dark brown sugar, packed

4 large eggs

1 tsp vanilla extract

¼ cup (60 ml) bourbon

1 tsp angostura bitters

1⅓ cups (220 ml) light corn syrup

½ cup (115 g) butter, melted

3 tbsp (23 g) all-purpose flour

½ tsp kosher salt

2¼ cups (272 g) chopped pecans

Preheat the oven to 350°F (177°C, or gas mark 4). Line a 9 x 13 x 2-inch (23 x 33 x 5-cm) baking pan with parchment paper or nonstick foil.

In the bowl of a stand mixer fitted with the paddle attachment, cream together the butter and granulated sugar. Add the egg yolk and mix well. Add the flour and salt, and mix until well combined.

Pat the crust evenly into the bottom of the prepared pan. Prick the entire crust with the tines of a fork. Bake for 20 to 22 minutes until the crust is a light golden brown.

Increase the oven temperature to 400°F (204°C, or gas mark 6).

In a large bowl, whisk together the brown sugar, eggs, vanilla, bourbon, bitters and corn syrup. Add the melted butter and whisk until smooth. Add the flour and salt, and whisk until completely combined. Fold the chopped pecans into the batter. Pour over the warm crust and bake for 10 minutes.

Reduce the heat to 350°F (177°C, or gas mark 4). Bake for 30 minutes until the filling is golden brown and puffed. Allow to cool completely before cutting into squares.

BITTERS BREAD PUDDING WITH BOURBON–BITTERS SAUCE

When my best friend of over twenty-five years recently got married, she turned to me to make her dessert buffet. One of the items that had to be included was her mom's New Orleans bread pudding; Deborah's version is studded with raisins and served with a decadent bourbon sauce. This is my version of bread pudding with bourbon-soaked dried cherries and angostura bitters, which I recently made for Deborah to much praise.

YIELD: 12 SERVINGS

1 (16-oz [454-g]) loaf French bread, preferably a day old
2 cups (473 ml) whole milk
2 cups (473 ml) heavy cream
1 cup (120 g) dried cherries
½ cup (120 ml) bourbon
4 large eggs, beaten
1 cup (192 g) sugar
1 tbsp (15 ml) vanilla extract
1 tsp angostura bitters
1 tsp ground cinnamon
1 tbsp (10 g) orange zest
3 tbsp (43 g) butter, melted

BOURBON-BITTERS SAUCE
½ cup (115 g) butter
1 cup (220 g) dark brown sugar, packed
¼ tsp kosher salt
1 large egg, beaten
¼ cup (60 ml) bourbon
½ tsp angostura bitters

Cut the bread into 1-inch (2.5-cm) cubes and place them in a large bowl. Pour the milk and cream over the bread and soak for 1 hour, stirring occasionally to make sure all the bread pieces are submerged in the liquid. Place the dried cherries and bourbon in a small bowl, and let sit while the bread is soaking.

Add the eggs, sugar, vanilla, bitters, cinnamon, orange zest and cherries with the bourbon to the bread-milk mixture. Stir well to combine.

Preheat the oven to 375°F (191°C, or gas mark 5). Pour the melted butter into a glass or ceramic 9 x 13 x 2-inch (23 x 33 x 5-cm) baking pan. Pour the bread pudding mixture into the pan. Bake for 50 minutes until the top is golden brown.

While the bread pudding is baking, melt together the butter, brown sugar and salt in a small saucepan. Whisk in the beaten egg and continue cooking on low heat, stirring constantly, until the sauce is thickened, 2 to 3 minutes. Remove from the heat, and add the bourbon and bitters. Serve the sauce warm over the bread pudding.

CHAPTER THREE

Flowers and Herbs

One of my earliest baking memories is sitting at the kitchen table with my Dad. He was teaching me to make baklava. When the dessert finished baking, he poured syrup made with rose water over the hot pastry, perfuming the entire kitchen. My infatuation with floral desserts was forged. This chapter uses both floral and fresh herbal ingredients to create bold, uniquely flavored desserts.

CRANBERRY-ROSEMARY MUFFINS

Many years ago I bought a cranberry-rosemary muffin in a local LA coffee shop. The brown sugar muffin batter was studded with bright cranberry jam and flecks of fresh rosemary. It was one of the most unusual and delicious muffins I had ever eaten. This recipe was created out of necessity when I learned that the shop stopped carrying them. I like to think mine are even better than the muffins from the coffee shop.

YIELD: 18 MUFFINS

⅔ cup (160 ml) vegetable oil

1 cup (237 ml) whole milk

2 large eggs

1 tbsp (10 g) orange zest

1 cup (220 g) dark brown sugar, packed

2¼ cups (281 g) all-purpose flour

1 tbsp (11 g) baking powder

½ tsp kosher salt

1 tbsp (4 g) chopped, fresh rosemary

1 cup (320 g) Cranberry Jam with Port Vinegar (page 108) or jarred cranberry sauce

TOPPING

¾ cup (165 g) dark brown sugar, packed

1 cup (125 g) all-purpose flour

1 tsp ground cinnamon

¼ tsp kosher salt

½ cup (115 g) butter, melted

GLAZE

½ cup (65 g) powdered sugar

2 tbsp (30 ml) orange juice

Preheat the oven to 375°F (191°C, or gas mark 5). Line a muffin pan with paper liners.

In a small bowl, combine the vegetable oil, milk, eggs and orange zest. In a large bowl, whisk together the brown sugar, flour, baking powder, salt and rosemary. Add the wet ingredients and mix until just combined. Gently fold the cranberry jam into muffin batter. Fill the prepared muffin cups ¾ full with batter.

Make the streusel topping by mixing together the brown sugar, flour, cinnamon, salt and melted butter. Mix until combined and crumbly.

Crumble approximately 1 tablespoon (15 g) of streusel topping on top of each muffin. Bake for 20 to 25 minutes until the muffins are golden brown and a cake tester inserted in the center of the muffin comes out clean.

While the muffins are baking, prepare the glaze by whisking together the powdered sugar and orange juice until smooth. Allow the muffins to cool for 5 minutes, then drizzle with glaze.

STRAWBERRY-BASIL "POP-TARTS"

There are always scrap pieces of pie dough left over whenever I make a pie. I repurpose the dough into rectangular hand pies filled with whatever jam I have in the fridge, so my kids can each have their own mini-pie. They are finished with a cream-powdered sugar glaze and sprinkles reminiscent of our favorite breakfast toaster pastry. They have become such a favored dessert in my house that I no longer wait for pie-dough scraps to make them. These are filled with a homemade strawberry-basil jam, but any jam can be used.

YIELD: 8 "POP-TARTS"

2¼ cups (281 g) all-purpose flour

3 tbsp (36 g) sugar

½ tsp kosher salt

¾ cup (172 g) cold butter, cut into ½-inch (1-cm) pieces

8 tbsp (118 ml) ice cold water

STRAWBERRY-BASIL JAM

4 cups (606 g) chopped, ripe strawberries

2 cups (384 g) sugar

2 tbsp (30 ml) fresh lemon juice

1 tbsp (14 g) butter

2 tbsp (5 g) chopped, fresh basil

GLAZE

½ cup (65 g) powdered sugar, sifted

3 tbsp (44 ml) heavy cream

¼ tsp vanilla extract

Multi-colored nonpareils

Combine the flour, sugar and salt in the bowl of a food processor. Pulse 5 to 8 times to combine the dry ingredients. Add the cold butter, pulsing until the mixture resembles coarse crumbs. Add the water to the flour-butter mixture and pulse until moist clumps form. The mixture will not form a ball of dough.

Combine the strawberries, sugar, lemon juice and butter in a medium saucepan over medium-high heat. Bring to a boil, stirring until the sugar has dissolved, about 5 minutes. Clip a digital, instant-read thermometer on the side of the saucepan and cook the jam for 10 to 15 minutes, stirring occasionally, until the temperature reaches 220°F (104°C). Remove from the heat and stir in the basil. Allow to cool completely before using. Jam can be stored in the refrigerator for up to 1 month.

Turn the dough onto a lightly floured surface and press into a disk. Roll the dough to ⅛-inch (3-mm) thickness, and cut into sixteen 3 x 4-inch (7½ x 10-cm) rectangles. Line a baking sheet with parchment paper. Place 8 rectangles of pie dough on the baking sheet, top each rectangle with 1 tablespoon (20 g) strawberry-basil jam. Top with a second rectangle of dough, and crimp around all sides with the tines of a fork.

Using a small, sharp knife, cut 3 small slits in the top of each pie. Place in the refrigerator for 15 minutes. While the pies are chilling, preheat the oven to 425°F (218°C, or gas mark 7). Bake the pies for 20 to 22 minutes until the pastries are a deep golden brown. Allow to cool to room temperature.

In a small bowl, whisk together the powdered sugar, heavy cream and vanilla until smooth. Frost the cooled pies with approximately 2 teaspoons (10 ml) of glaze and sprinkle with nonpareils.

BLUEBERRY–LEMON VERBENA BARS

While gardening in my backyard, I came across a fragrant plant that was new to me. After a thorough investigation and asking multiple friends, I learned that it was a large patch of lemon verbena. So, of course, I needed to bake with it. The bright, herbal lemon flavor pairs beautifully with blueberries in this almond-studded cookie bar.

YIELD: 16 BARS

1 cup (90 g) sliced almonds

1½ cups (187 g) all-purpose flour

¼ cup (21 g) ground almonds

½ cup (96 g) granulated sugar

½ cup (110 g) dark brown sugar, packed

2 tsp (7 g) fresh lemon zest

½ tsp kosher salt

¾ cup (172 g) cold butter, cut into ½-inch (1-cm) pieces

2 egg yolks

1 tsp vanilla extract

¾ cup (240 g) Blueberry–Lemon Verbena Jam

BLUEBERRY–LEMON VERBENA JAM

4 cups (600 g) fresh blueberries

2 cups (384 g) granulated sugar

2 tbsp (30 ml) fresh lemon juice

1 tbsp (14 g) butter

¼ cup (11 g) chopped fresh lemon verbena

Preheat the oven to 375°F (191°C, or gas mark 5). Line an 8 x 8 x 2-inch (20 x 20 x 5-cm) baking pan with parchment paper or nonstick foil.

Place the almonds in a medium frying pan and toast over medium heat, stirring constantly, until golden brown, about 5 to 7 minutes. Make sure to watch carefully as nuts can go from perfectly toasted to burnt very quickly. Set aside to cool.

In the bowl of an electric mixer, combine the flour, ground almonds, granulated sugar, brown sugar, lemon zest and salt. Mix to combine. With the mixer on low speed, add the butter one piece at a time. Continue to mix until the mixture resembles coarse crumbs. Add the egg yolks and vanilla, and mix until dough forms. Separate 1 cup (230 g) of dough into a small bowl and mix in toasted almond slices for the bar topping.

Combine the blueberries, granulated sugar, lemon juice and butter in a medium saucepan over medium-high heat. Bring to a boil, stirring until the sugar has dissolved, for 5 minutes. Clip a digital, instant-read thermometer on the side of the saucepan and cook the jam for 10 to 15 minutes, stirring occasionally, until the temperature reaches 220°F (104°C). Remove from the heat and stir in the lemon verbena. Allow to cool completely before using. Jam can be stored in refrigerator for up to 1 month.

Press the remaining dough into the prepared pan. Spread the jam over the bottom crust and crumble the topping evenly over the jam. Bake for 25 to 30 minutes until the jam is bubbling and the top is golden brown. Cool completely before cutting into squares.

BLACKBERRY—ROSE GERANIUM POUND CAKE

This cake was inspired by a seasonal donut at my favorite donut shop. The combination of tart blackberries and the floral, sweet rose geranium is addictive. I use rose geranium essential oil, a very concentrated flavor, in this recipe. To measure the small amount needed in both the cake and glaze recipes, I use a medicine dropper that is commonly used for dosing children's medicine. They can be bought from any drugstore or pharmacy. I always have one in my collection of measuring spoons!

YIELD: 8 TO 10 SERVINGS

1½ cups (187 g) all-purpose flour

1 tsp baking powder

½ tsp kosher salt

¾ cup (172 g) butter, room temperature

1½ cups (288 g) sugar

1 tsp vanilla extract

⅛ tsp rose geranium essential oil

3 large eggs

½ cup (118 ml) buttermilk, room temperature

1½ cups (227 g) fresh blackberries, cut in half

GLAZE

¼ cup (38 g) fresh blackberries

2 tbsp (30 ml) water

⅛ tsp rose geranium essential oil

Pinch of kosher salt

1½ cups (195 g) powdered sugar

Preheat the oven to 350°F (177°C, or gas mark 4). Grease a 9 x 5 x 3-inch (23 x 13 x 5-cm) loaf pan with nonstick cooking spray.

Combine the flour, baking powder and salt in a small bowl. In the bowl of a stand mixer fitted with the paddle attachment, cream together the butter, sugar, vanilla and rose geranium oil on medium speed for 5 to 7 minutes. The mixture will be light, fluffy and very pale yellow.

Add the eggs, one at a time, mixing after each addition. With the mixer on low speed, add the flour mixture, beating until just combined. Add the buttermilk and mix. Remove the bowl from the electric mixer and fold the blackberries into the batter with a rubber spatula.

Pour into the prepared pan. Bake for 60 to 70 minutes until a cake tester inserted in the center of the cake comes out clean.

While the cake is baking, place the blackberries and water in a small bowl and purée using an immersion blender. Add the rose geranium oil, salt and powdered sugar. Whisk until combined.

Cool the cake in the pan for 15 minutes before turning out onto a cooling rack to cool completely. Once cool, pour glaze over the top of the cake allowing it to drizzle down the sides.

ORANGE BLOSSOM–MARMALADE CAKE

This cake evokes the spectacular smell of the orange trees in my garden when they are in full bloom. There is something magical every year when the orange blossoms appear on the tree and the air is intensely perfumed with their scent. This is a "naked" cake, which means that the sides of the cake are not frosted, allowing you to see the layers of cake and frosting.

YIELD: 10 TO 12 SERVINGS

1 cup (237 ml) buttermilk, room temperature

½ tsp baking soda

3¼ cups (406 g) all-purpose flour

½ tsp kosher salt

1 tbsp (11 g) baking powder

1 cup (230 g) butter, room temperature

1½ cups (288 g) sugar

3 large eggs

1 cup (320 g) orange marmalade

2 tbsp (30 ml) orange blossom water

1 tbsp (10 g) fresh orange zest

FROSTING

4 oz (113 g) cream cheese, room temperature

½ cup (115 g) butter, room temperature

¼ cup (80 g) orange marmalade

2 tsp (10 ml) orange blossom water

½ tsp kosher salt

2½ cups (325 g) powdered sugar, sifted

Preheat the oven to 350°F (177°C, or gas mark 4). Line the bottoms of three 9-inch (23-cm) round cake pans with parchment paper and spray them with nonstick cooking spray.

In a small bowl, combine the buttermilk and baking soda. The mixture may get bubbly. In another bowl, whisk together the flour, salt and baking powder.

In the bowl of a stand mixer fitted with the paddle attachment, cream together the butter and sugar until light and fluffy, approximately 2 minutes. Add the eggs, one at a time, mixing well after each addition, and scraping the sides and bottom of the bowl with a rubber spatula.

Add the marmalade, orange blossom water and orange zest. Mix well. Add the dry ingredients in 2 additions, alternating with the buttermilk-soda mixture, and mixing well after each addition.

Divide the batter evenly among the prepared cake pans. Bake for 20 to 25 minutes, until the cake is golden brown and a cake tester inserted into the middle of each cake comes out clean. Cool the cakes in their pans for 10 minutes before removing from the pans and cooling completely on a wire rack.

In the bowl of an electric mixer fitted with the paddle attachment, cream together the cream cheese and butter until light and fluffy. Add the marmalade, orange blossom water and salt. Mix to combine. Add the powdered sugar and mix on low speed until incorporated. Increase the mixer speed to high and whip for 2 minutes, until the frosting is light and fluffy.

To frost the cake, place one layer on a serving plate and spread with ⅓ of the frosting—making sure to spread the frosting to the edges, but not on the sides of the cakes. Repeat with the remaining 2 layers.

ROSE PANNA COTTA WITH RASPBERRY GELÉE

Panna cotta is a traditional Italian dessert made with cream, sugar and gelatin. It is a lovely summer dessert that can be made without turning on the oven. I first tasted the combination of rose and raspberry while eating my way through every macaron shop in Paris, and I immediately fell in love with the flavors together. This would also make a fabulous, sexy dessert for Valentine's Day.

YIELD: 8 SERVINGS

1 (2½-tsp [12-g]) packet unflavored gelatin

3 tbsp (45 ml) cold water

2 cups (473 ml) heavy cream

¼ cup (48 g) sugar

Pinch of kosher salt

¾ tsp rose water

GELÉE

1½ cups (184 g) fresh raspberries

¼ cup (48 g) sugar

½ tsp fresh lime juice

1½ tsp (7 g) unflavored gelatin

3 tbsp (45 ml) cold water

In a very small saucepan or a metal, 1-cup (237-ml) measuring cup, sprinkle the gelatin over the water. Let it sit for 1 minute to bloom and soften the gelatin. Heat the mixture over low heat until the gelatin is dissolved and the mixture is a liquid, 1 to 2 minutes. Remove from the heat.

In a medium saucepan, combine the heavy cream, sugar and salt. Bring to just a boil over medium-high heat, stirring to dissolve the sugar, 3 to 5 minutes. Remove from the heat, and add the dissolved gelatin mixture and rose water.

Divide the cream among eight 4-ounce (113-g) mason jars or glasses. Chill in the refrigerator until set, approximately 4 hours.

When the panna cotta is nearly set, make the gelée. Using an immersion blender or a blender, purée together the raspberries, sugar and lime juice. Pour the purée through a fine-mesh sieve. Place the raspberry purée in a small saucepan and bring to just a boil over medium-high heat.

In a very small saucepan or a metal, 1-cup (237-ml) measuring cup, sprinkle the gelatin over the water. Let it sit for 1 minute to bloom and soften the gelatin. Heat the mixture over low heat until the gelatin is dissolved and the mixture is a liquid, 1 to 2 minutes. Remove from the heat and add to the warmed raspberry purée.

Once the panna cotta is set, evenly divide the raspberry gelée over the top of each. Chill in the refrigerator until the gelée is set, approximately 2 hours.

LAVENDER CARAMEL SAUCE

Lavender subtly perfumes this caramel sauce that is poured over my Brown Sugar and Lavender Bitters Pots de Crème (page 40). It pairs beautifully served with a scoop of chocolate ice cream, drizzled over a room-temperature piece of Brie or spooned into a warm cup of earl grey tea.

YIELD: APPROXIMATELY 1¾ CUPS (574 G)

1 cup (192 g) sugar
⅓ cup (79 ml) light corn syrup
⅓ cup (79 ml) water
¼ tsp kosher salt
1 cup (237 ml) heavy cream
⅓ cup (76 g) butter, room temperature
2 tbsp (4 g) dried lavender

Combine the sugar, corn syrup, water and salt in a medium saucepan. Bring to a boil over medium-high heat, stirring until the sugar has dissolved, 5 minutes. Reduce the heat to medium-low and continue to cook until the sugar is a dark, golden brown, 10 to 15 minutes, and the mixture reaches 300°F (149°C) on an instant-read thermometer.

Brush the inside walls of the pan with water to prevent sugar crystallization. Remove from the heat and add the heavy cream. The mixture will bubble up and the sugar will harden.

Return the pan to the heat. Whisk until the sugar melts, the mixture comes to a boil, 2 to 5 minutes, and the caramel is smooth. Remove from the heat. Whisk in the butter and lavender.

Allow the lavender to steep in the caramel for 10 to 15 minutes. Pour the warm caramel through a fine-mesh strainer into a clean container. Pour the caramel into jars and store in the refrigerator for up to 2 months.

CHERRY-TARRAGON SCONES

I love the combination of sweet-tart cherries and the slight licorice notes of tarragon. I was introduced to this flavor combination when trying a cherry-tarragon soda, and I knew I needed to use it in a dessert. These scones are fabulous eaten with a great cup of coffee, or they can be used to make cherry shortcakes with fresh Whipped Cream (page 147) and Cherry Balsamic Sauce (page 108).

YIELD: 8 SCONES

2 cups (250 g) all-purpose flour

⅓ cup (64 g) sugar

1 tbsp (11 g) baking powder

½ tsp kosher salt

½ cup (76 g) dried cherries, coarsely chopped

1 tsp chopped, fresh tarragon

½ cup (115 g) cold butter, cut into ½-inch (1-cm) cubes

¾ cup plus 2 tbsp (207 ml) heavy cream, divided

4 tsp (18 g) raw sugar

Preheat the oven to 400°F (204°C, or gas mark 6). Line a baking sheet with parchment paper.

Combine the flour, sugar, baking powder, salt, cherries and tarragon in a large bowl. Add the diced butter. Using your fingers or a pastry cutter, cut the butter into the flour mixture until the butter is the size of small peas. Add ¾ cup (177 ml) of heavy cream, and stir until the ingredients are just moistened and come together.

Turn the dough out onto a lightly floured surface and pat into an 8-inch (20-cm) round. Cut into 8 equal wedges and place on the prepared baking sheet.

Brush the top of each scone with the remaining 2 tablespoons (30 ml) heavy cream, and sprinkle each with approximately ½ teaspoon of raw sugar. Bake for 15 to 18 minutes until the scones are golden brown.

FRESH MINT CHEESECAKE

I planted three small mint plants in one of my planter boxes about three years ago, hoping to have a little fresh mint to use in drinks and recipes. It soon took over the entire planter box and continues to spread, and now I have A LOT of fresh mint to use up! Do not expect this sophisticated mint cheesecake to taste like peppermint ice cream or candy canes. It has a lovely fresh mint flavor that is accented by the use of Branca Menta, a bitter amaro liquor that contains both peppermint and menthol.

YIELD: 12 TO 16 SERVINGS

1½ cups (135 g) chocolate-mint sandwich-cookie crumbs, approximately 20 cookies

1 cup (237 ml) heavy cream

1 oz (28 g) fresh mint, washed

2 lb (907 g) full-fat cream cheese, room temperature

1½ cups (288 g) sugar

½ tsp kosher salt

5 large eggs

6 tbsp (90 ml) Branca Menta

Preheat the oven to 350°F (177°C, or gas mark 4). Wrap the outside of a 9-inch (23-cm) round springform pan with a double thickness of aluminum foil, making sure there are no holes in the foil.

Pat the cookie crumbs into the bottom of the springform pan, and bake for 12 to 15 minutes. Cool completely while making the cheesecake filling. Reduce the oven to 325°F (163°C, or gas mark 3).

Combine the heavy cream and mint in a small saucepan, and bring to a boil over medium heat. Reduce the heat to low and simmer for 5 minutes. Remove the pan from the heat, and let the cream and mint steep for 30 minutes. Pour the heavy cream through a fine-mesh sieve into a clean bowl, pressing on the mint to extract oils and flavor.

Place the cream cheese, sugar and salt in the bowl of a food processor. Mix until well blended. Add the eggs and process until smooth. Add the infused cream and Branca Menta.

Pour the filling into the crust. Place the springform pan into a large roasting pan and pour enough hot water into the roasting pan to come halfway up the sides of springform pan. Bake for 1 hour and 10 minutes until the cheesecake is just set in the center.

Turn the oven off, keep the door closed and let the cheesecake stand in the oven for 1 hour. Remove the cheesecake from the water bath and cool completely to room temperature. Refrigerate for 6 hours to overnight.

LAVENDER SHORTBREAD

These buttery shortbreads are studded with lavender and dark chocolate. To finely chop the dried lavender, I use a spice grinder or a very clean coffee grinder.

YIELD: 25 COOKIES

¾ cup (172 g) butter, room temperature

½ cup (96 g) sugar

¼ tsp kosher salt

¾ tsp finely chopped dried lavender

2 tsp (10 ml) vanilla extract

1¾ cups (219 g) all-purpose flour

¼ cup (45 g) chopped bittersweet chocolate

1 tbsp (12 g) sanding sugar

Preheat the oven to 350°F (177°C, or gas mark 4). Line baking sheets with parchment paper.

In the bowl of a stand mixer fitted with the paddle attachment, cream together the butter, sugar, salt, lavender and vanilla. Add the flour and chocolate, and mix on low speed until dough comes together.

Place the dough onto a lightly floured surface and shape into a disk. Wrap in plastic wrap and refrigerate for 30 minutes. Roll the dough on a lightly floured surface to a 10 x 10-inch (25 x 25-cm) square.

Cut into twenty-five 2 x 2-inch (5 x 5-cm) squares. Place the cookies on the prepared baking sheets. Sprinkle the tops with sanding sugar. Bake for 13 to 15 minutes until the edges of the cookies are golden brown. Cool completely.

BLUEBERRY-THYME CHEESECAKE PARFAITS

A lovely steak dinner to celebrate a friend's birthday was followed with a disappointing and flavorless "deconstructed cheesecake." I made the bold statement that I could create a much better dessert. The gauntlet was thrown down, and I had to follow through. This is my response to that challenge, and my friends have declared it a winner. The lemony thyme complements the blueberries in the compote, and it accents the rich, creamy cheesecake filling.

YIELD: 6 SERVINGS

1 cup (90 g) graham cracker crumbs
1 tbsp (12 g) sugar
¼ tsp kosher salt
4 tbsp (57 g) butter, melted

FILLING
8 oz (227 g) full-fat cream cheese, room temperature
8 oz (227 g) mascarpone cheese, room temperature
½ cup (96 g) sugar
¼ cup (59 ml) heavy cream
1 tsp vanilla extract
¼ tsp kosher salt

BLUEBERRY-THYME COMPOTE
12 oz (340 g) fresh blueberries
½ cup (96 g) sugar
1 tbsp (15 ml) lemon juice
1 tsp chopped fresh thyme

Preheat the oven to 350°F (177°C, or gas mark 4). Line a baking sheet with parchment paper.

In a medium bowl, stir together the graham cracker crumbs, sugar and salt. Add the melted butter and stir until the crumbs are evenly coated. Pour the crumbs onto the prepared pan, and bake for 10 minutes until the crumbs are golden brown. Cool completely to room temperature.

In the bowl of a stand mixer fitted with the paddle attachment, cream together the cream cheese, mascarpone and sugar until smooth. Add the heavy cream, vanilla and salt, and whip for 2 minutes.

Mix together the blueberries, sugar, lemon juice and thyme in a medium saucepan. Bring to a boil over medium-high heat, stirring to make sure the sugar is dissolved. Reduce the heat to medium-low. Cook until the berries burst and release their juices and the sauce thickens, approximately 10 to 15 minutes. Remove from the heat and cool completely to room temperature.

Place 1 tablespoon (4 g) of crumb mixture in the bottoms of six 8-ounce (227-g) mason jars or glasses, top with approximately 2 tablespoons (30 g) of cheesecake mixture and then 1 tablespoon (15 g) of compote. Repeat the layers and top with about ½ tablespoon (2 g) of crumb mixture. Refrigerate for 30 minutes or up to 4 hours before serving.

WALNUT-CARDAMOM BAKLAVA WITH ROSE SYRUP

This recipe is inspired by my early memories of making baklava with my dad. There were never any measurements because he learned how to make it from his mom who did everything by eye. My family always made their baklava with walnuts and soaked it in a rose-scented syrup when the pastry was hot out of the oven. Keep the filo dough covered while working to prevent it from drying out and breaking.

YIELD: 24 SQUARES

1 (16-oz [454-g]) package frozen filo dough, thawed

6 cups (696 g) walnuts

¾ cup (144 g) sugar

1 tsp ground cinnamon

1 tsp ground cardamom

1½ cups (344 g) butter, melted

ROSE SYRUP

2 cups (384 g) sugar

1 cup (237 ml) water

Pinch of kosher salt

½ tsp rose water

Preheat the oven to 350°F (177°C, or gas mark 4).

Unroll the filo dough. It should measure approximately 12 x 17-inches (30 x 43-cm). Cut the stack of pastry in half to get 2 stacks of pastry that measure 8½ x 12-inches (21 x 30-cm). Cover the stacks of filo with plastic wrap or a damp kitchen towel.

Combine the walnuts, sugar, cinnamon and cardamom in the bowl of a food processor. Process the mixture until the nuts are finely ground. Transfer the nut mixture to a large bowl.

Brush a 9 x 13 x 2-inch (23 x 33 x 5-cm) baking pan with melted butter. Place 1 sheet of filo in the pan and brush with melted butter. Repeat the layering and buttering with 11 more sheets of filo for a total of 12 layers. Spread half of the nut filling evenly over the filo in the pan. Repeat the layering of filo dough and butter for a total of 8 more layers of filo. Spread with the remaining nut filling. Repeat the layering of filo dough and butter for a total of 10 more layers of filo. Using a sharp knife, cut through the top layer of filo dough, cutting the baklava into 24 pieces. Bake for 45 minutes until the baklava is a deep golden brown.

Combine the sugar, water and salt in a medium saucepan. Bring to a boil over medium-high heat, stirring until the sugar dissolves. Reduce the heat to medium and boil until the syrup is slightly reduced, approximately 5 minutes. Remove from the heat and allow to cool to room temperature. Once cooled, add the rose water and stir well.

Pour the rose syrup over the hot baklava. Cool to room temperature.

CHAPTER FOUR

Spices

Traditional baking spices add a familiar flavor to desserts. This chapter explores using spices more commonly associated with savory dishes—such as cumin, curry, garam masala, cardamom, turmeric, star anise, chili and Chinese five-spice powder—to create delicious, unusual and bold flavors in desserts.

CURRIED OATMEAL COOKIES

One of my kids' favorite dinners is a chicken curry that I serve with a variety of condiments. I sat one night, watching my kids pile dried mango chunks and toasted coconut on their dinners and an idea was born. These curried oatmeal cookies have pieces of soft, dried mango and toasted, shredded coconut nestled in a cookie dough with the added warmth of curry and ginger. This unusual dessert combination will soon become addictive!

YIELD: 4 DOZEN COOKIES

2 cups (250 g) all-purpose flour

1 tsp baking soda

½ tsp kosher salt

1 tsp ground ginger

1 tsp Indian curry powder

1 cup (230 g) butter, room temperature

1½ cups (330 g) dark brown sugar, packed

½ cup (96 g) granulated sugar

1 tsp vanilla extract

2 large eggs

2½ cups (201 g) rolled oats

1 cup (150 g) diced, dried mango

1 cup (76 g) sweetened, shredded coconut, toasted

Preheat the oven to 375°F (191°C, or gas mark 5). Line baking sheets with parchment paper.

In a small bowl, whisk together the flour, baking soda, salt, ginger and curry powder. In the bowl of an electric mixer, combine the butter, brown sugar, granulated sugar and vanilla. Cream together on low for 1 minute, scraping down the sides and bottom of the bowl with a rubber spatula.

Increase the mixer speed to high and cream the butter-sugar mixture for 5 minutes. The mixture will become very light colored and fluffy. Add the eggs, one at a time, mixing well after each addition.

With the mixer on low speed, add the dry ingredients. Add the rolled oats, mango and coconut. Mix on low speed until the mixture is well combined.

Using a ¾-ounce (22-g) cookie scoop (purple handled) place the cookie dough onto the prepared baking sheets. Bake for 10 to 12 minutes until the edges of the cookies are golden brown and the centers are just set. The centers of the cookies will look slightly underbaked, but they will become firm upon cooling. Cool the cookies on the baking sheets for 5 minutes before removing.

CUMIN-SPICED PECANS

The use of cumin and cayenne in these sweet-spicy pecans accents the rich, nutty flavor of the pecans. Be warned that these nuts are addictive. I created them to use in my banana bread recipe, but they often don't make it into the batter! Make a double (or even triple) batch so you have enough for snacking, gift giving, adding to salads and for using in banana bread.

YIELD: APPROXIMATELY 2½ CUPS (300 G)

10 oz (284 g) pecan halves
2 tbsp (29 g) butter, melted
2 tbsp (28 g) dark brown sugar, packed
1 tsp ground cinnamon
½ tsp ground cumin
¼ tsp cayenne pepper
1 tsp kosher salt

Preheat the oven to 300°F (149°C, or gas mark 2). Line a baking sheet with parchment paper.

Toss together the pecans and melted butter. Add the brown sugar, cinnamon, cumin, cayenne and salt, and then mix well, making sure the nuts are evenly coated.

Pour the nuts onto the baking sheet. Bake for 20 minutes, stirring after 10 minutes. Cool completely to room temperature.

BANANA BREAD WITH CUMIN-SPICED PECANS

This has been my go-to banana bread recipe for years. My children frequently refuse to eat fresh bananas in my house, letting them brown instead so that I will make them this bread. The use of sour cream in the batter creates a moist bread with a slight tang. The Cumin-Spiced Pecans (page 83) add a burst of spice and heat that complements the banana. This batter can also be baked in two 9-inch (23-cm) round cake pans and then frosted with Brown Sugar–Cream Cheese Frosting (page 99) for a delicious banana cake.

YIELD: 8 TO 10 SERVINGS

½ cup (115 g) butter, room temperature

1 cup (192 g) sugar

2 large eggs

1 tsp vanilla extract

1 cup (230 g) mashed, ripe bananas (approximately 2–3 bananas)

½ cup (60 g) sour cream, room temperature

1½ cups (187 g) all-purpose flour

1 tsp baking soda

1 tsp kosher salt

1 cup (121 g) chopped, Cumin-Spiced Pecans (page 83)

Preheat the oven to 350°F (177°C, or gas mark 4). Grease a 9 x 5 x 3-inch (23 x 13 x 8-cm) loaf pan with nonstick cooking spray.

In the bowl of a stand mixer fitted with the paddle attachment, cream together the butter and sugar until light and fluffy, about 1 minute. Add the eggs, one at a time, mixing after each addition. Add the vanilla, mashed bananas and sour cream, mixing well to combine.

Add the flour, baking soda and salt to the butter-banana mixture. Mix until the ingredients are just combined. Fold the pecans into the batter, and pour the batter into the prepared pan.

Bake for 50 to 60 minutes until the top is golden brown and a cake tester inserted in the center of the bread comes out clean. Cool completely before cutting.

CARDAMOM-GINGER APPLE CAKE WITH BROWN SUGAR GLAZE

I was first introduced to cardamom as a child while visiting my paternal grandmother Teta. She made sweet, strong, Arabic coffee scented with cardamom. In this recipe, the rich, earthy cardamom pairs with warm ginger and apples to create a cake that tastes like fall and reminds me of the warmth of my grandmother's home.

YIELD: 12 TO 16 SERVINGS

3 cups (375 g) all-purpose flour

1 tsp baking soda

2 tsp (5 g) ground cardamom

½ tsp ground ginger

½ tsp kosher salt

1¼ cups (298 ml) canola oil

½ cup (60 g) sour cream, room temperature

1¼ cups (275 g) dark brown sugar, packed

½ cup (96 g) granulated sugar

3 large eggs

2 tsp (10 ml) vanilla extract

2 cups (450 g) grated, peeled apple, approximately 3 medium apples

2 cups (300 g) diced, peeled apple, approximately 2 medium apples

SYRUP

½ cup (118 ml) apple cider

½ cup (96 g) sugar

5 cardamom pods, crushed

BROWN SUGAR GLAZE

½ cup (110 g) dark brown sugar, packed

⅓ cup (78 ml) heavy cream

¼ cup (57 g) butter, room temperature

¼ tsp kosher salt

½ tsp vanilla extract

¾ cup (98 g) powdered sugar

Preheat the oven to 350°F (177°C, or gas mark 4). Grease an 8-cup (1-kg) Bundt pan with nonstick cooking spray.

In a medium bowl, whisk together the flour, baking soda, cardamom, ginger and salt. In the bowl of a stand mixer fitted with the paddle attachment, combine the oil, sour cream, brown sugar, granulated sugar, eggs and vanilla. Mix on medium speed until well combined and the mixture is smooth. Add all of the apples.

Add the flour mixture and mix on low speed until the ingredients are well combined, scraping the sides and bottom of the bowl.

Pour the batter into the prepared pan. Bake for 45 to 50 minutes until a cake tester inserted in center of the cake comes out clean.

While the cake is baking, make the syrup. Combine the apple cider, sugar and cardamom pods in a small saucepan. Bring to a boil, stirring to ensure all the sugar is dissolved, 3 to 5 minutes. Remove from the heat and allow the cardamom pods to steep in the syrup for 15 minutes. Strain through a fine-mesh sieve.

With the cake still in the pan, poke holes into the cooked cake using a thin wood or metal skewer. While the cake is still hot from the oven, pour syrup over the top, allowing it to soak into the cake. Allow the cake to sit in the pan, absorbing the syrup for 10 minutes before turning out to cool completely on a cooling rack.

Whisk together the brown sugar, heavy cream, butter and salt in a medium saucepan. Bring the mixture to a boil over medium-high heat, whisking constantly. Once the mixture comes to a boil and the butter is melted, remove from the heat and pour into a medium bowl. Cool to room temperature. Add the vanilla and powdered sugar, and whisk until smooth. The glaze will be thick and glossy.

Pour the glaze over the top of the cake, allowing it to drizzle down the sides.

CHINESE FIVE-SPICE "NICKERDOODLES"

When my son, Nicky, was about five years old, I was making snickerdoodles and he was looking at the recipe as I was making them. He suddenly declared that they were HIS cookies because his name was included in the name of the cookies. These favorite cookies have since been called Nickerdoodles in my home. I use Chinese five-spice powder—a blend of cinnamon, star anise, ginger, cloves and Szechuan peppercorn—in place of the cinnamon traditionally used. I love the spicy, warm flavors that the five-spice gives these cookies.

YIELD: APPROXIMATELY 3 DOZEN COOKIES

2½ cups (312 g) all-purpose flour

2 tsp (6 g) cream of tartar

1 tsp baking soda

½ tsp kosher salt

½ cup (115 g) butter, room temperature

½ cup (110 g) solid vegetable shortening, room temperature

1½ cups (288 g) sugar

1 tsp vanilla extract

2 large eggs

2 tbsp (15 g) Chinese five-spice powder

½ cup (96 g) sugar

Preheat the oven to 375°F (191°C, or gas mark 5). Line baking sheets with parchment paper.

Whisk together the flour, cream of tartar, baking soda and salt. In the bowl of a stand mixer fitted with the paddle attachment, cream together the butter, shortening, sugar and vanilla until light and fluffy, approximately 2 minutes. Add the eggs, one at a time, mixing well after each addition.

Add the flour mixture and mix until well combined, scraping the sides and bottom of the bowl with a rubber spatula. In a medium bowl, whisk together the five-spice powder and sugar.

Scoop the cookie dough using a ¾-ounce (22-g) scoop (purple handled), rolling each ball of dough in the sugar-spice mixture before placing on the prepared baking sheets. Bake for 10 to 12 minutes until the edges of the cookies are golden brown and the top of the cookies are slightly cracked.

GARAM MASALA— ZUCCHINI CAKE WITH MOLASSES GLAZE

One evening, I was making chicken tikka masala and I was struck by the thought that garam masala would be a delicious addition to desserts. Every Indian family has their own blend of garam masala. The typical ingredients are a combination of black peppercorns, mace, cinnamon, cloves, brown and green cardamom and nutmeg—all spices that complement the flavor of zucchini. You can find garam masala in the grocery store spice section or at Indian supermarkets.

YIELD: 12 TO 16 SERVINGS

2 cups (250 g) all-purpose flour

2 tsp (9 g) baking soda

1 tsp baking powder

1 tsp kosher salt

3 tsp (8 g) garam masala

3 large eggs

1¼ cups (296 ml) vegetable oil

¾ cup (144 g) granulated sugar

¾ cup (165 g) dark brown sugar, packed

1 tsp vanilla extract

2 cups (220 g) grated, unpeeled zucchini, approximately 2 medium zucchinis

MOLASSES GLAZE

½ cup (120 ml) molasses

¼ cup (57 g) butter

½ cup (118 ml) heavy cream

¼ tsp kosher salt

1 cup (130 g) powdered sugar, sifted

Preheat the oven to 350°F (177°C, or gas mark 4). Grease an 8-cup (1-kg) Bundt pan with nonstick cooking spray.

In a medium bowl, whisk together the flour, baking soda, baking powder, salt and garam masala. Combine the eggs, vegetable oil, granulated sugar, brown sugar, vanilla and zucchini in the bowl of a stand mixer. Mix using the paddle attachment on medium speed until well combined.

Add the flour mixture. Mix on low speed until the ingredients are well combined, scraping the sides and bottom of the bowl with a rubber spatula.

Pour the batter into the prepared pan. Bake for 40 to 45 minutes until a cake tester inserted in center of the cake comes out clean. Allow the cake to cool in the pan for 10 minutes before turning out to cool completely on a cooling rack.

Whisk together the molasses, butter, heavy cream and salt in a medium saucepan. Bring the mixture to a boil over medium-high heat, whisking constantly. Once the mixture comes to a boil and the butter is melted, 3 to 5 minutes, remove from the heat and pour into a medium bowl. Cool to room temperature. Add the powdered sugar and whisk until smooth. The glaze will be thick and glossy.

Pour the glaze over the top of the cake, allowing it to drizzle down the sides of the cake.

STAR-ANISE MOLASSES COOKIES

I have been making these molasses cookies for many years, and I include them in my annual Christmas cookie platter that I give out to friends. I have been told by numerous people that they wait ALL YEAR for them. These cookies have a crispy exterior with a soft, chewy center, and they are coated in crunchy, sparkly sugar. The star anise adds a warm, faint licorice note to the traditional spices used in these cookies.

YIELD: APPROXIMATELY 3 DOZEN COOKIES

2½ cups (312 g) all-purpose flour

2 tsp (9 g) baking soda

1 tsp kosher salt

1 tsp ground star anise

1 tsp ground ginger

1 tsp ground cinnamon

¼ cup (57 g) butter, room temperature

½ cup (110 g) solid vegetable shortening, room temperature

1 cup (220 g) dark brown sugar, packed

1 large egg

½ cup (120 ml) dark molasses

⅓ cup (80 g) diced, crystallized ginger

½ cup (96 g) coarse or sanding sugar

In a small bowl, whisk together the flour, baking soda, salt, star anise, ground ginger and cinnamon.

In the bowl of a stand mixer fitted with the paddle attachment, combine the butter, vegetable shortening and brown sugar. Cream together on medium for 2 minutes, scraping down the sides and bottom of the bowl with a rubber spatula. Add the egg and molasses, mixing until well combined.

With the mixer on low speed, add the dry ingredients. Mix in the crystallized ginger. Cover the bowl with plastic wrap, and refrigerate the dough for 1 to 2 hours.

Preheat the oven to 350°F (177°C, or gas mark 4). Line baking sheets with parchment paper.

Scoop the cookie dough with a ¾-ounce (22-g) scoop (purple handled), rolling each ball of dough in the coarse sugar. Place the dough on the prepared baking sheets. Bake for 9 to 11 minutes until the edges of the cookies are set and the centers begin to crack. The centers of the cookies will look slightly underbaked, but they will firm upon cooling. Cool the cookies on baking sheets for 5 minutes before removing.

GINGER-PEACH TURNOVERS

Many of my friends have given me the nickname of "The Boozy Baker" because many of my flavor combinations and desserts are inspired by cocktails. This dessert is no exception—the filling evoking a Bourbon Peach Smash. Store-bought puff pastry makes these turnovers a quick dessert to make.

YIELD: 12 PASTRIES

2 sheets of frozen puff pastry, thawed

2 cups (360 g) diced, peeled peaches, approximately 2–3 medium peaches

¼ cup (55 g) dark brown sugar, packed

1 tbsp (9 g) cornstarch

¼ tsp ground ginger

¼ tsp kosher salt

1 tbsp (15 g) chopped, crystallized ginger

1 tbsp (15 ml) bourbon

2 tbsp (30 ml) heavy cream

2 tbsp (25 g) raw sugar

Preheat the oven to 400°F (204°C, or gas mark 6). Line baking sheets with parchment paper.

On a lightly floured surface, roll each sheet of puff pastry out to a 15 x 10-inch (38 x 25-cm) rectangle. Cut each rectangle into six 5 x 5-inch (13 x 13-cm) squares for a total of 12 puff pastry squares. Place the pastry on the prepared baking sheets and refrigerate while making the filling.

In a large bowl, toss together the peaches, brown sugar, cornstarch, ground ginger, salt, crystallized ginger and bourbon. Remove the pastry squares from the refrigerator and place a heaping tablespoon (13 g) of filling in the middle of each square.

Brush the edges of the pastry square with water. Fold the pastry over the filling diagonally to create a triangle-shaped turnover. Press together the pastry edges using the tines of a fork. Brush the tops of each turnover with heavy cream and sprinkle with raw sugar. Bake for 20 to 25 minutes until the turnovers are puffed and a deep golden brown.

STAR-ANISE STICKY TOFFEE PUDDING

Sticky toffee pudding, a traditional British dessert, is one of my favorite winter desserts. The date-spice cake is doused with warm toffee sauce, creating a decadent dessert. I have added ground star anise to my recipe because I love the combination of dates, brown sugar and anise. Serve this cake with lightly sweetened Whipped Cream (page 147) or homemade Vanilla Ice Cream (page 147).

YIELD: 8 SERVINGS

1¼ cups (189 g) chopped, pitted dates, approximately 15 Medjool dates

1 cup (237 ml) water

1 tsp baking soda

½ cup (115 g) butter, room temperature

½ cup (96 g) granulated sugar

½ cup (110 g) dark brown sugar, packed

1 tsp vanilla extract

3 large eggs

1½ cups (187 g) all-purpose flour

1 tsp baking powder

½ tsp kosher salt

1½ tsp (4 g) ground star anise

SAUCE

1 cup (220 g) dark brown sugar, packed

2 cups (473 ml) heavy cream

¼ cup (57 g) butter

½ tsp kosher salt

½ tsp vanilla extract

1 tbsp (15 ml) bourbon

Preheat the oven to 350°F (177°C, or gas mark 4). Line a 9-inch (23-cm) round cake pan with parchment paper. Grease the pan and parchment paper with nonstick cooking spray.

Combine the chopped dates and water in a medium saucepan. Bring to a boil over medium heat, about 3 to 5 minutes. Once the mixture has boiled, remove from the heat and stir in the baking soda. The mixture will bubble and thicken. Let cool to room temperature.

In the bowl of a stand mixer fitted with the paddle attachment, cream together the butter, granulated sugar, brown sugar and vanilla until light and fluffy. Add the eggs, one at a time, scraping the sides and bottom of the bowl with a rubber spatula after each addition. Add the cooled date mixture and mix. Add the flour, baking powder, salt and star anise, and mix until just combined.

Pour the batter into the prepared pan. Bake for 28 to 30 minutes until a cake tester inserted into the center of the cake comes out clean. While the cake is cooling to room temperature, prepare the sauce.

Combine the brown sugar, heavy cream, butter and salt in a medium saucepan. Bring to a boil over medium heat, stirring occasionally. Reduce the heat to low. Simmer for 15 to 20 minutes until the sauce is slightly reduced and thickened. Remove from the heat, and stir in the vanilla and bourbon.

Serve each slice of cake with a generous pour of warm sauce.

CUMIN CARROT CAKE WITH BROWN SUGAR— CREAM CHEESE FROSTING

One of my favorite fall vegetable dishes is roasted carrot with cumin and brown sugar, so I've transferred these savory flavors into a carrot cake. The cumin-scented cake layers are dotted with sweet, golden raisins and toasted pecans, and each layer is frosted with a brown sugar–cream cheese frosting.

YIELD: 10 TO 12 SERVINGS

1¼ cups (296 ml) vegetable oil

1 cup (192 g) granulated sugar

1 cup (220 g) dark brown sugar, packed

2 tsp (10 ml) vanilla extract

4 large eggs

4 cups (680 g) grated carrots

2 cups (250 g) all-purpose flour

1½ tsp (4 g) ground cumin

1 tsp ground cinnamon

2 tsp (8 g) baking powder

1 tsp baking soda

1 tsp kosher salt

1 cup (151 g) golden raisins

1 cup (121 g) chopped, toasted pecans

BROWN SUGAR–CREAM CHEESE FROSTING

8 oz (227 g) full-fat cream cheese, room temperature

1 cup (230 g) butter, room temperature

1 cup (220 g) dark brown sugar, packed

¼ tsp kosher salt

1 tsp vanilla extract

3½ cups (455 g) powdered sugar, sifted

Preheat the oven to 350°F (177°C, or gas mark 4). Line the bottoms of three 9-inch (23-cm) round cake pans with parchment paper and spray with nonstick cooking spray.

In the bowl of a stand mixer fitted with a paddle attachment, mix together the vegetable oil, granulated sugar, brown sugar, vanilla and eggs. Add the carrots and mix until incorporated. Add the flour, cumin, cinnamon, baking powder, baking soda, salt, raisins and pecans. Mix until well combined.

Divide the batter evenly among the prepared pans. Bake for 25 minutes until golden brown and a cake tester inserted into the middle of each cake comes out clean. Cool the cakes in their pans for 10 minutes before removing from the pans and cooling completely on a wire rack.

In the bowl of a stand mixer fitted with the paddle attachment, cream together the cream cheese, butter, brown sugar and salt until the brown sugar is dissolved, approximately 1 to 2 minutes. Add the vanilla and powdered sugar. Mix on low speed until incorporated, then increase the mixer speed to high and whip for 2 minutes until the frosting is light and fluffy.

To frost the cake, place one layer on a serving plate and spread evenly with ¼ of the frosting. Place the second layer on top and spread evenly with another ¼ of the frosting. Place the last layer on top of the cake, and spread the top and sides with the remaining frosting.

MEXICAN HOT CHOCOLATE CAKE

This chocolate cake has all the flavors of Mexican hot chocolate with chipotle and ancho chili powders, which add a smoked chili flavor, and a touch of cayenne to add an extra kick. The cake comes together quickly in one bowl. Pair a slice of this cake with a cup of coffee spiked with añejo tequila for a fabulous flavor combination!

YIELD: 10 TO 12 SERVINGS

2 cups (250 g) all-purpose flour

2 cups (384 g) sugar

1 tsp baking powder

2 tsp (9 g) baking soda

1 tsp kosher salt

¾ cup (83 g) unsweetened cocoa powder

1 tsp ground cinnamon

1 tsp chipotle chili powder

1 tsp ancho chili powder

¼ tsp cayenne pepper

1 cup (237 ml) whole milk

1 cup (237 ml) vegetable oil

1 cup (237 ml) warm water

2 eggs

FROSTING

1 cup (180 g) milk chocolate chips

1 cup (180 g) bittersweet chocolate chips

1 cup (121 g) sour cream, room temperature

2 tsp (10 ml) vanilla extract

¼ tsp kosher salt

¼ tsp ground cinnamon

Preheat the oven to 350°F (177°C, or gas mark 4). Line the bottoms of three 9-inch (23-cm) round cake pans with parchment paper and spray with nonstick cooking spray.

In a large bowl, whisk together the flour, sugar, baking powder, baking soda, salt, cocoa powder, cinnamon, chipotle powder, ancho powder and cayenne. Add the milk, vegetable oil, water and eggs. Whisk until well combined.

Divide the batter evenly among the prepared pans. Bake for 22 to 25 minutes until a cake tester inserted into the middle of each cake comes out clean. Cool the cakes in their pans for 10 minutes before removing from the pans and cooling completely on a wire rack.

Place the milk chocolate chips and bittersweet chocolate chips in a medium glass bowl. Microwave at 30-second increments, stirring after each increment, to melt the chocolate. The chocolate should be melted in 90 seconds to 2 minutes. Add the sour cream, vanilla, salt and cinnamon, and stir until combined and the frosting is creamy. Use the frosting immediately to frost the cake as it will thicken upon cooling.

To frost the cake, place one layer on a serving plate and spread evenly with ¼ of the frosting. Place the second layer on top and spread evenly with another ¼ of the frosting. Place the last layer on top of the cake, and spread the top and sides with the remaining frosting.

CURRIED PUMPKIN PIE WITH BRÛLÉED SUGAR TOPPING

As crazy as it might sound, I am not a huge fan of pumpkin pie—or I wasn't until I developed this recipe. Indian curry powders can contain a variety of different spices, but most are a mixture of cumin, turmeric, coriander, chili pepper, cardamom, ginger, cloves, nutmeg, cinnamon and black pepper—all spices that complement and elevate the flavor of pumpkin. After the pie is baked and cooled, it is topped with sugar that is caramelized with a kitchen torch; the sugar provides a sweet crunch before reaching the creamy pumpkin custard.

YIELD: 8 SERVINGS

1¼ cups (156 g) all-purpose flour

1 tbsp (12 g) sugar

½ tsp kosher salt

½ cup (115 g) cold butter, diced

3–4 tbsp (45–60 ml) ice cold water

1 tsp apple cider vinegar

4 tbsp (48 g) superfine sugar

FILLING

3 large eggs

½ cup (110 g) dark brown sugar, packed

1½ cups (270 g) canned pumpkin purée

1½ cups (355 ml) heavy cream

1 tsp vanilla extract

½ tsp kosher salt

1½ tsp (4 g) curry powder

¼ tsp ground turmeric

½ tsp ground cinnamon

¼ tsp ground ginger

¼ cup (57 g) butter, melted and cooled

Combine the flour, sugar and salt in the bowl of a food processor. Pulse 5 to 8 times to combine the dry ingredients. Add the cold butter, pulsing until the mixture resembles coarse crumbs. Add the water and apple cider vinegar to the flour-butter mixture. Pulse until moist clumps form; the mixture will not form a ball of dough.

Turn the dough onto a lightly floured surface and press into a disk. Roll out the dough on a lightly floured surface into a 13-inch (33-cm) round. Place into a 9½ -inch (24-cm), deep-dish pie pan and decoratively crimp edges of the pie. Refrigerate for 30 minutes.

Preheat the oven to 350°F (177°C, or gas mark 4). In a large bowl, whisk together the eggs. Add the brown sugar, pumpkin, heavy cream, vanilla, salt, curry powder, turmeric, cinnamon and ginger. Whisk until well combined. Stir in the melted and cooled butter; it may clump a little after adding, but it will melt into the filling during baking. Place the unbaked pie crust on a parchment-lined baking sheet and pour the filling into the crust.

Bake for 40 to 45 minutes until the edges of the pie are set and the center has a slight jiggle. Cool to room temperature and then refrigerate for at least 2 hours to overnight.

When ready to serve the pie, sprinkle the superfine sugar over the top of the pie. Use a kitchen blowtorch to evenly melt and caramelize the sugar. Allow the caramelized sugar to cool and harden for approximately 5 minutes before serving.

CHINESE FIVE-SPICE OLD-FASHIONED DONUTS

Old-fashioned donuts are traditionally flavored with nutmeg, and they are completely coated in a vanilla glaze that gets into every nook and cranny of the donut. My donuts are flavored with the warm flavors of Chinese five-spice powder and are coated in a bourbon glaze. I'm of the opinion that a warm donut should be enjoyed at any time of the day and not only with a cup of coffee in the morning!

YIELD: 12 DONUTS AND 12 HOLES

2¼ cups (281 g) all-purpose flour

1½ tsp (6 g) baking powder

1 tsp kosher salt

½ tsp Chinese five-spice powder

2 tbsp (29 g) butter, room temperature

½ cup (96 g) sugar

2 egg yolks

¾ cup (91 g) sour cream, room temperature

Vegetable oil, for frying

GLAZE

3 cups (390 g) powdered sugar

¼ cup plus 2 tbsp (89 ml) hot water

2 tbsp (30 ml) bourbon

½ tsp vanilla extract

¼ tsp kosher salt

In a small bowl, whisk together the flour, baking powder, salt and five-spice powder. In the bowl of a stand mixer fitted with the paddle attachment, cream together the butter and sugar. Add the egg yolks and mix until fluffy. Add the sour cream and mix well. Add the dry ingredients and mix until just combined. Cover the dough with plastic wrap and refrigerate for 1 hour.

On a lightly floured surface, roll the dough to ½-inch (1.5-cm) thickness. Using a donut cutter or a 3-inch (8-cm) and 1-inch (2.5-cm) round biscuit cutter, cut out donuts and place them on a lightly floured baking tray.

In a medium bowl, add the powdered sugar, hot water, bourbon, vanilla and salt. Whisk together until the sugar is completely dissolved and the glaze is smooth. Set aside.

Clip an instant-read thermometer to the side of a heavy bottomed, deep pot and pour 2 to 3 inches (5 to 8 cm) of vegetable oil into it. Heat the oil to 345°F (174°C). Fry the donuts a few at a time, cooking for about 3 minutes on each side. Remove the cooked donuts from the oil and place onto a baking sheet lined with paper towel to drain.

Allow the cooking oil to return to 345°F (174°C) before frying the next batch of donuts and holes. Let the donuts cool for 5 to 10 minutes before immersing each donut into the glaze. Set the glazed donuts on a wire rack placed over a baking sheet. Let sit for 20 to 30 minutes until the glaze has hardened.

CHAPTER FIVE

Vinegars

I am slightly obsessed with the abundance of delicious and interesting vinegars. I cannot walk by a vinegar stall at the farmer's market without stopping and tasting every single one, and frequently I walk away with a few newly purchased bottles. In this chapter, both traditional and flavored vinegars are used to make delicious pastries that are accented and balanced by the flavors and acidity of vinegars.

CRANBERRY JAM WITH PORT VINEGAR

I created this cranberry jam to use in my Cranberry-Rosemary Muffin recipe (page 54), but the uses for it are endless. Serve it as a side to your Thanksgiving turkey, roasted chicken or roasted pork tenderloin. Or substitute it for the Blueberry-Thyme Compote in the Cheesecake Parfaits (page 74). Make a double batch and keep it in your fridge for all your cranberry sauce needs! The use of port vinegar in this recipe accents the natural tartness and deep flavor of the cranberries.

YIELD: APPROXIMATELY 3 CUPS (900 G)

12 oz (340 g) fresh or frozen cranberries

½ cup (76 g) dried cranberries

1 tbsp (10 g) orange zest

½ cup (118 ml) orange juice

2 cups (384 g) sugar

2 tbsp (30 ml) port vinegar

Combine the fresh and dried cranberries, orange zest, orange juice, sugar and port vinegar in a medium saucepan. Bring to a boil over medium-high heat, and boil for 5 minutes.

Reduce the heat to low. Continue to simmer until the cranberries burst and the jam starts to thicken, approximately 10 to 15 minutes. Cool the jam and refrigerate for up to 1 month.

CHERRY BALSAMIC SAUCE

I originally developed this sauce to accompany the Chocolate Old-Fashioned Cake (page 44), but have since found many other uses for it. It makes a delicious cherry shortcake when paired with the Cherry-Tarragon Scones (page 69), and it is decadent poured warm over a scoop of Vanilla Ice Cream (page 147). I use frozen cherries in the recipe because they are always available and are already pitted, but definitely substitute fresh cherries when they are in season!

YIELD: APPROXIMATELY 2 CUPS (700 G)

1 (16-oz [454-g]) bag frozen sweet cherries, thawed

¾ cup (144 g) sugar

1 tbsp (10 g) fresh orange zest

⅓ cup (80 ml) fresh orange juice

¼ cup (60 ml) cherry balsamic vinegar or aged balsamic vinegar

Pinch of kosher salt

Combine the cherries, sugar, orange zest, orange juice, balsamic vinegar and salt in a medium saucepan. Bring to a boil, then reduce the heat to medium. Continue to cook until the cherries have broken down and released their juices and the sauce thickens, approximately 10 to 15 minutes. Cool completely. The sauce can be stored in the refrigerator for up to 1 month.

BERRY CRISP WITH BLACKBERRY BALSAMIC VINEGAR

I spent many childhood summers with my maternal grandmother in Washington state, helping her pick raspberries from the numerous bushes in her yard. I would occasionally be rewarded for my hard work with a raspberry crisp and vanilla ice cream. A fruit crisp definitely ranks as one of my all-time favorite desserts. The topping for this crisp uses a combination of spelt and oat flours, which results in a nutty flavor and also makes the dish gluten-free. You can substitute all-purpose flour and experiment with different combinations of fruit.

YIELD: 16 SERVINGS

¾ cup (98 g) spelt flour

½ cup (65 g) oat flour

1¼ cups (101 g) old-fashioned oats

1¼ cups (275 g) dark brown sugar, packed

1 tsp ground cinnamon

½ tsp kosher salt

½ cup (115 g) cold butter, cubed

FILLING

4 cups (604 g) fresh blackberries

4 cups (592 g) fresh blueberries

4 cups (492 g) fresh raspberries

1 cup (192 g) granulated sugar

¼ cup (60 ml) blackberry balsamic vinegar

4 tbsp (38 g) cornstarch

In the bowl of a stand mixer fitted with the paddle attachment, combine the spelt flour, oat flour, oats, brown sugar, cinnamon and salt. Mix to combine. Add the butter, and mix on medium speed until the mixture is combined and crumbly.

Preheat the oven to 350°F (177°C, or gas mark 4). Butter a 9 x 13 x 2-inch (23 x 33 x 5-cm) glass or ceramic baking dish.

In a large bowl, toss together the berries, granulated sugar, balsamic vinegar and cornstarch. Pour into the prepared baking dish. Crumble the topping evenly over the fruit filling.

Bake for 45 to 50 minutes until the fruit filling is bubbly and the topping is golden brown. Serve warm or at room temperature.

PEAR-GORGONZOLA TARTS WITH PORT VINEGAR GLAZE

Sweet pears, funky-salty Gorgonzola and port are a classic savory flavor combination that I have converted into a delicious dessert. Enjoy these tarts with a glass of port. Using store-bought puff pastry in this recipe makes it a quick dessert.

YIELD: 6 INDIVIDUAL TARTS

1 piece of store-bought puff pastry, defrosted

2 oz (57 g) cream cheese, room temperature

1 oz (28 g) Gorgonzola, room temperature

1 tbsp (15 ml) honey

3 large firm, ripe pears

3 tsp (12 g) sugar

PORT VINEGAR GLAZE

2 tbsp (30 ml) honey

2 tbsp (30 ml) port vinegar

Preheat the oven to 375°F (191°C, or gas mark 5). Line a baking sheet with parchment paper.

On a lightly floured surface, roll the puff pastry to a 15 x 10-inch (39 x 25-cm) rectangle. Cut the puff pastry into six 5 x 5-inch (13 x 13-cm) squares. Place the pastry squares on the prepared tray and refrigerate while preparing the filling.

Combine the cream cheese, Gorgonzola and honey in a medium bowl. Mix together using a whisk or hand mixer until fluffy and well combined. Dollop approximately 1 tablespoon (20 g) of filling in the center of each pastry square.

Peel the pears and cut them in half along the longitude of the pear. Remove the core and slice each half horizontally, keeping each pear half together. Using a spatula, place a pear half on each pastry square, fanning the pear out over the Gorgonzola filling. Sprinkle the top of each pear with ½ teaspoon of sugar.

Bake for 22 to 25 minutes until the edges of the tart are a deep golden brown.

While the cooked tarts are cooling, whisk together the honey and port vinegar in a small saucepan. Bring to a boil over medium heat. Remove from the heat.

Allow the tarts to cool for 5 minutes. Brush the top of each tart with glaze.

SUGAR COOKIES WITH CHERRY BALSAMIC FROSTING

Living in Seattle during the "coffee-revolution," I saw coffee-carts on practically every street corner. It seemed that every cart sold "pink cookies"—a large, soft, buttery sugar cookie frosted with a generous amount of pink, sweet, cherry-flavored frosting. These cookies are my version of the pink cookie, with a frosting that is less sweet and more tart-cherry. I use some of the delicious syrup that comes with my favorite cocktail cherries to flavor these cookies.

YIELD: 24 LARGE COOKIES

1⅓ cups (445 g) butter, room temperature
1½ cups (288 g) sugar
2 tsp (10 ml) vanilla extract
2 large eggs
3½ cups (437 g) all-purpose flour
2 tsp (8 g) baking powder
½ tsp kosher salt

CHERRY BALSAMIC FROSTING

1 cup (230 g) butter, room temperature
4 cups (521 g) powdered sugar
3 tbsp (45 ml) cherry syrup
3 tbsp (45 ml) cherry balsamic vinegar
3 tbsp (45 ml) heavy cream
¼ tsp kosher salt
¼ tsp red food coloring

Preheat the oven to 350°F (177°C, or gas mark 4). Line baking sheets with parchment paper.

In the bowl of a stand mixer fitted with the paddle attachment, cream together the butter, sugar and vanilla until light and fluffy, approximately 2 minutes. Add the eggs, one at a time, mixing well after each addition.

Add the flour, baking powder and salt. Mix until well combined, scraping the sides and bottom of the bowl with a rubber spatula. Scoop the cookie dough with a 1⅓-ounce (38 g) scoop (red handled) onto the prepared baking trays and gently press each ball of dough with your hand to flatten slightly.

Bake for 10 to 12 minutes until the edges of the cookies are golden brown. Cool completely.

In the bowl of a stand mixer fitted with the paddle attachment, mix together the butter, powdered sugar, cherry syrup, balsamic vinegar, heavy cream, salt and food coloring on low speed until combined. Increase the mixer to high and beat for 1 to 2 minutes, until the frosting is light and fluffy.

Frost each cookie generously with the cherry frosting, using approximately 1 to 1½ tablespoons (1 to 2 g) of frosting per cookie.

PEACH AND WHITE BALSAMIC VINEGAR COBBLER

This cobbler is one of my go-to peach recipes every summer. It is both fast and delicious! I like to leave the peach skin on the peaches in this dish because I like the color and texture they provide. The white balsamic vinegar adds a floral acidity to the sweet peaches and buttery cake. Serve warm with a huge scoop of homemade Vanilla Ice Cream (page 147).

YIELD: 8 TO 12 SERVINGS

½ cup (118 ml) butter, melted

1 cup (125 g) all-purpose flour

1½ cups (288 g) sugar, divided

1 tbsp (11 g) baking powder

¼ tsp kosher salt

1 cup (237 ml) whole milk

6 cups (1 kg) fresh peach slices, approximately 4 large peaches

2 tbsp (30 ml) white balsamic vinegar

Preheat the oven to 375°F (191°C, or gas mark 5). Pour melted butter into a glass or ceramic 9 x 13 x 2-inch (23 x 33 x 5-cm) baking dish.

In a medium bowl, whisk together the flour, 1 cup (192 g) of sugar, baking powder and salt. Add the milk and mix to combine. Pour the batter over the melted butter in the baking dish—do not mix!

Combine the peach slices, vinegar and remaining ½ cup (96 g) of sugar in a medium saucepan. Bring to a boil over medium-high heat, stirring to make sure the sugar is dissolved, about 5 minutes. Remove from the heat and dollop the peach mixture over the top of the batter.

Bake for 25 to 30 minutes until the cobbler is golden brown and bubbly.

PLUM BALSAMIC CRUMBLE PIE

My son Gavin is my fruit monster. He will devour any type of fruit at any time of the day, but his favorite is definitely plums. If I can manage to hide a few plums from him, I make this pie. The earthy sweetness of the plums is accented by the tart, rich balsamic vinegar, and the plums are topped with almond flecked, brown sugar–crumble topping. Needless to say, I also have to hide this pie from my fruit monster.

YIELD: 8 SERVINGS

1¼ cups (156 g) all-purpose flour

1 tbsp (12 g) granulated sugar

½ tsp kosher salt

½ cup (115 g) cold butter, diced

3–4 tbsp (45–60 ml) ice cold water

1 tsp apple cider vinegar

FILLING

6 cups (1 kg) sliced plums, approximately 8–10 medium plums

½ cup (110 g) dark brown sugar, packed

2 tbsp (30 ml) balsamic vinegar

2 tbsp (19 g) cornstarch

TOPPING

⅓ cup (64 g) granulated sugar

¼ cup (55 g) dark brown sugar, packed

½ cup plus 2 tbsp (78 g) all-purpose flour

2 tsp (5 g) ground cinnamon

¼ tsp kosher salt

½ cup (115 g) cold butter, cut into small dice

½ cup (42 g) flaked almonds

Combine the flour, granulated sugar and salt in the bowl of a food processor. Pulse 5 to 8 times to combine the dry ingredients. Add the cold butter, pulsing until the mixture resembles coarse crumbs. Add the water and apple cider vinegar to the flour-butter mixture. Pulse until moist clumps form; the mixture will not form a ball of dough.

Turn the dough onto a lightly floured surface and press into a disk. Roll out the dough on a lightly floured surface into a 13-inch (33-cm) round. Place into a 9½-inch (23-cm) pie dish and decoratively crimp edges of the pie. Refrigerate for 30 minutes.

Preheat the oven to 350°F (177°C, or gas mark 4).

Toss the plums with brown sugar, balsamic vinegar and cornstarch. Pour the filling into the refrigerated pie crust.

In a medium bowl, stir together the granulated sugar, brown sugar, flour, cinnamon and salt. Blend in the butter with your fingers until the mixture forms small clumps. Stir in the almonds. Crumble the streusel evenly over the plum filling.

Place the pie on a parchment-lined baking sheet. Bake for 50 to 55 minutes until the crust and top of pie are golden and the filling is bubbling.

RUSTIC APPLE TART WITH APPLE CIDER VINEGAR GLAZE

I liken this tart to a cross between an apple cookie and apple pie. The super-thin, buttery crust is topped with thinly sliced apples that caramelize while baking, and it is finished with the tartness of the apple cider vinegar glaze. I generously say this will yield 8 servings, but I've eaten the entire tart with a friend on more occasions than I'd like to admit!

YIELD: 8 SERVINGS

1¼ cups (156 g) all-purpose flour

⅓ cup (30 g) slivered almonds

1 tbsp (12 g) sugar

½ tsp kosher salt

½ cup (115 g) cold butter, diced

4 tbsp (60 ml) ice cold water

1 tsp apple cider vinegar

TOPPING

2 Granny Smith apples, peeled and cored

¼ cup (48 g) sugar

2 tbsp (29 g) cold butter, cut into pea-sized cubes

APPLE CIDER VINEGAR GLAZE

2 tbsp (30 ml) unfiltered apple cider vinegar

2 tbsp (24 g) sugar

Combine the flour, slivered almonds, sugar and salt in the bowl of a food processor. Pulse 5 to 8 times to combine the dry ingredients. Add the cold butter, pulsing until the mixture resembles coarse crumbs. Add the water and apple cider vinegar to the flour-butter mixture. Pulse until moist clumps form; the mixture will not form a ball of dough.

Turn the dough onto a lightly floured surface and press into a rectangle. Roll out the dough into a 9 x 12-inch (23 x 30-cm) rectangle. Place the dough onto a greased, parchment-lined baking sheet and refrigerate for 30 minutes.

Preheat the oven to 400°F (204°C, or gas mark 6).

Cut the apples in half, lengthwise. Place each half flat onto a cutting board. Cut each apple half into thin, horizontal slices making sure to keep each apple half together. Remove the pastry rectangle from the refrigerator and evenly fan the slices of each apple in 4 rows across the pastry. Sprinkle the sugar over the top of the apples and dot with the butter.

Bake for 30 minutes until the sugar has caramelized over the apples and the edges of the apples are golden brown.

While the tart is baking, combine the apple cider vinegar and sugar in a small saucepan. Bring to a boil over medium heat, stirring to make sure the sugar is dissolved, about 2 to 4 minutes. Remove from the heat.

Allow to cool for 5 minutes and brush the top of the tart with the apple cider vinegar glaze.

CHAPTER SIX

Salts

Salt is a necessary ingredient in any dessert or pastry. It balances and rounds out the flavors. I began experimenting with different salts as accents in my desserts after eating my first chocolate chip cookie with a sprinkle of crunchy, flaked sea salt: the salt balances the sweetness and adds depth to the chocolate in the cookie. This chapter uses flaked, smoked and flavored salts to create bold, salty-sweet desserts.

BROWN-BUTTER CHOCOLATE CHIP COOKIES WITH SMOKED SALT

I believe that these are the perfect chocolate chip cookies—with crisp edges and a chewy center, full of both dark and milk chocolate and finished with a crunch of smoked salt. The butter is browned before use, adding a toasty-nutty flavor to the cookies. Chilling the cookie dough before baking is critical for both the flavor and texture of the cookies—so although it will be hard to wait, don't skip this step!

YIELD: 30 COOKIES

1 cup (230 g) butter

2¼ cups (281 g) all-purpose flour

1¼ tsp (5 g) baking soda

½ tsp kosher salt

1¼ cup (275 g) dark brown sugar, packed

¼ cup (48 g) granulated sugar

1 large egg

1 egg yolk

2 tsp (10 ml) vanilla extract

1 tbsp (8 g) sour cream

1 cup (180 g) semi-sweet chocolate chips

1 cup (180 g) milk chocolate chips

Smoked salt (such as smoked Maldon or smoked Jacobsen)

Melt the butter in a saucepan over medium heat. Whisk the butter as it melts and begins to brown. Continue whisking the butter until it gives off a nutty aroma and is golden brown, 5 to 7 minutes. Pour the browned butter into the bowl of a stand mixer fitted with the paddle attachment and allow it to cool for 10 minutes.

While the butter is cooling, whisk together the flour, baking soda and salt in a small bowl. Add the brown sugar and granulated sugar to the brown butter in the mixer bowl, and mix on medium speed until well combined. Beat in the egg, egg yolk, vanilla and sour cream. Add the dry ingredients. Mix on low speed until just combined. Add the chocolate chips and mix briefly to just incorporate.

Line a baking sheet with parchment. Using a 1-ounce (28-g) scoop (black handled), scoop balls of cookie dough onto the baking sheet. You can scoop the dough close together because you will transfer the dough to new sheets to bake. Wrap with plastic wrap and refrigerate for at least 2 hours or overnight.

Preheat the oven to 350°F (177°C, or gas mark 4). Place the cookie dough onto parchment-lined baking sheets, leaving a 1-inch (2.5-cm) space between cookies.

Sprinkle the top of each cookie with a large pinch of smoked salt. Bake for 10 to 12 minutes until the edges of the cookies are set and lightly browned. The center of the cookies will look slightly underbaked, but they will firm upon cooling. Cool the cookies on the baking sheets for 5 minutes before removing.

SALTED CARAMEL SAUCE

This salted caramel sauce is the base for many of the desserts in this chapter. It is delicious poured warm over ice cream, added to a cup of coffee, used as a dip for apples or eaten straight out of the jar. I usually make a double batch to have in my fridge at all times.

YIELD: APPROXIMATELY 2¼ CUPS (740 G)

1½ cups (288 g) sugar
¼ cup (60 ml) light corn syrup
¼ cup (60 ml) water
1 cup (237 ml) heavy cream
¼ cup (30 g) crème fraîche or sour cream
½ tsp Maldon salt
1 tsp vanilla extract

Combine the sugar, corn syrup and water in a medium saucepan. Bring to a boil over medium-high heat, stirring until the sugar has dissolved, 5 minutes. Reduce the heat to medium-low. Continue to cook until the sugar is a dark, golden brown, 10 to 15 minutes, and the mixture reaches 300°F (149°C) on an instant-read thermometer.

Brush the inside walls of the pot with water to prevent sugar crystallization. Remove from the heat and add the heavy cream. The mixture will bubble up and the sugar will harden.

Return the pan to the heat. Whisk until the sugar melts, 2 to 5 minutes, the mixture comes to a boil, and the caramel is smooth. Remove from the heat and allow to cool for 30 to 45 minutes.

Add the crème fraîche, salt and vanilla to the cooled caramel, and whisk until well combined. Pour into jars and store in the refrigerator for up to 2 months.

NECTARINE AND BLACKBERRY ALMOND CAKES WITH LEMON SALT

These cakes are based on yet another of my favorite French pastries, the financier: a buttery almond cake that is traditionally eaten as an afternoon snack. You can top them with any seasonal fruit, but I especially love the combination of blackberries, nectarines, lemon and almond.

YIELD: 12 MINI CAKES

¾ cup (172 g) butter

1 cup (85 g) almond flour

1½ cups (195 g) powdered sugar, sifted

1 cup (125 g) all-purpose flour

¼ tsp kosher salt

6 large egg whites, room temperature

1 tsp vanilla extract

¼ tsp almond extract

24 fresh blackberries

1 nectarine, sliced into 12 pieces

½ tsp lemon salt

Preheat the oven to 400°F (204°C, or gas mark 6). Grease a 12-cup muffin pan with nonstick cooking spray.

Melt the butter in a saucepan over medium heat. Whisk the butter as it melts and begins to brown. Continue whisking the butter until it gives off a nutty aroma and is golden brown, 5 to 7 minutes. Remove from the heat and allow to cool to room temperature.

In a large bowl, whisk together the almond flour, powdered sugar, flour and salt. Stir in the egg whites, vanilla and the almond extract. Mix until smooth. Stir in the cooled brown butter, mixing until well combined.

Divide the batter evenly among the prepared muffin cups. Top each with 2 blackberries and 1 nectarine slice, and sprinkle each with lemon salt.

Bake at 400°F (204°C, or gas mark 6) for 8 minutes. Reduce the heat to 350°F (177°C, or gas mark 4) and bake for an additional 8 minutes. Turn the oven off and let the cakes sit in the oven for 5 minutes. Remove the cakes from the oven and allow to cool in the pan for 10 minutes.

PUMPKIN BREAD WITH ROSEMARY SALT

October 1st marks the beginning of pumpkin season in our house, and the first item that is requested is this moist, easy-to-make pumpkin bread. The fragrant rosemary salt accents the fall flavors of pumpkin pie spice and maple syrup. A delicious addition to this bread is ½ cup (75 g) of raisins mixed in with the toasted pecans.

YIELD: 8 TO 10 SERVINGS

1 cup (125 g) all-purpose flour
½ cup (110 g) dark brown sugar, packed
½ cup (96 g) granulated sugar
¾ tsp baking soda
1½ tsp (4 g) pumpkin pie spice
½ tsp kosher salt
2 large eggs
2 tbsp (30 ml) maple syrup
1 cup (180 g) canned pumpkin purée
⅓ cup (79 ml) vegetable oil
½ cup (60 g) pecans, toasted

ROSEMARY SALT
1 tsp flaked sea salt, such as Maldon
¼ tsp chopped, fresh rosemary

Preheat the oven to 350°F (177°C, or gas mark 4). Grease a 9 x 5 x 3-inch (23 x 13 x 8-cm) loaf pan with nonstick cooking spray.

In a large bowl, whisk together the flour, brown sugar, granulated sugar, baking soda, pumpkin pie spice and salt. Combine the eggs, maple syrup, pumpkin and oil in a medium bowl. Add the wet ingredients to the flour mixture. Stir well with a rubber spatula, scraping the sides and bottom of the bowl to make sure all of the ingredients are incorporated. Fold in the toasted pecans and pour into the prepared pan.

Mix together the salt and chopped rosemary, rubbing them together with your fingertips to release the oils in the rosemary.

Sprinkle the top of the batter with approximately ½ teaspoon of rosemary salt. Bake for 40 to 45 minutes until a cake tester inserted in the center of the loaf comes out clean. Cool completely before removing from the pan.

CHOCOLATE POUND CAKE WITH CHILI SALT

This moist chocolate cake is drizzled with a dark chocolate glaze and generously sprinkled with chili salt. The first bite of cake is a combination of chocolate and salt, followed by the gentle heat of the chili. It is fabulous with a cup of coffee as an afternoon snack or with a scoop of ice cream for dessert.

YIELD: 1 LOAF, OR 8 TO 10 SLICES

1 tsp instant espresso powder

½ cup (56 g) unsweetened cocoa powder

¼ cup (45 g) semi-sweet chocolate chips

½ cup (118 ml) boiling water

1 cup (230 g) butter, room temperature

¾ cup (144 g) granulated sugar

½ cup (110 g) dark brown sugar, packed

2 tsp (10 ml) vanilla extract

3 large eggs

½ cup (60 g) sour cream

1¼ cups (156 g) all-purpose flour

½ tsp kosher salt

½ tsp baking powder

¼ tsp baking soda

½ tsp chili salt

GLAZE

⅓ cup (80 ml) heavy cream

⅓ cup (60 g) semi-sweet chocolate chips

1 tbsp (14 g) butter, room temperature

Preheat the oven to 350°F (177°C, or gas mark 4). Grease a 9 x 5 x 3-inch (23 x 13 x 8-cm) loaf pan with nonstick cooking spray.

In a small bowl, combine the espresso powder, cocoa powder and chocolate chips. Pour boiling water over the mixture and let stand for 1 minute. Whisk the mixture to a smooth paste and allow to cool to room temperature. In the bowl of a stand mixer fitted with the paddle attachment, cream together the butter, granulated sugar, brown sugar and vanilla.

Continue mixing on high speed until the mixture is light and fluffy, approximately 5 minutes. With the mixer on low speed, add the cooled chocolate mixture, scraping down the sides and bottom of the bowl with a rubber spatula to ensure the mixture is well combined.

Add the eggs, one at a time, mixing well after each addition. Stir in the sour cream. Add the flour, salt, baking powder and baking soda, and mix on low until the ingredients are just combined. Pour the batter into the prepared loaf pan. Bake for 50 minutes until a toothpick inserted in the center of the loaf comes out clean.

Allow the cake to cool in the pan for 15 minutes before turning out onto a cooling rack to cool completely.

While the cake is cooling, make the glaze. In a small saucepan, bring the heavy cream to a boil. Remove the pan from the heat. Add the chocolate and let the mixture sit for 5 minutes before whisking. Add the butter, and whisk until completely combined and the glaze is smooth and glossy.

Pour the glaze over the top of the cooled cake and sprinkle with chili salt.

SMOKED SALT ALMOND THUMBPRINTS

My walk home from school every day took me by a Belgian chocolate shop, and every so often I would go into the store and buy one piece of marzipan covered in dark chocolate. That piece of candy would be devoured before I made it home. These almond cookies filled with dark chocolate ganache are my homage to those chocolates.

YIELD: 24 COOKIES

8 oz (227 g) almond paste
⅔ cup (87 g) powdered sugar
1 large egg white, room temperature
4 tbsp (60 ml) heavy cream
¼ cup (45 g) bittersweet chocolate chips
Smoked flaked salt, such as smoked Maldon

Preheat the oven to 325°F (163°C, or gas mark 3). Line baking sheets with parchment paper.

Break the almond paste into pieces and place them in the bowl of a stand mixer fitted with the paddle attachment. Add the powdered sugar and mix until mixture resembles coarse crumbs. Add the egg white and beat until the mixture is a thick paste.

Form teaspoon-sized balls of dough and place them onto the prepared baking sheets. Using your index finger, moistened with water, press an indentation into the center of each cookie.

Bake for 12 to 14 minutes until the edges of cookies are set and light golden brown. Using the end of a wooden spoon, re-indent the cookies. Cool completely.

In a small saucepan, bring the heavy cream to a boil. Remove the pan from the heat. Add the chocolate and let the mixture sit for 5 minutes before whisking until smooth. Dollop approximately ½ teaspoon of ganache into the center of each cookie and sprinkle with a few flakes of smoked salt.

SMOKY S'MORES BARS

S'mores are a year-round treat in my home: whether we are roasting marshmallows over a fire in the backyard or over the gas flame on my stove, or we are eating these delicious cookie bars. A filling of chocolate ganache is loaded with mini marshmallows and sits atop a graham cracker crust. The entire cookie is finished with a generous sprinkle of smoked salt to evoke the flavor of roasted marshmallows over a campfire.

YIELD: 24 BARS

1½ cups (135 g) graham cracker crumbs

½ cup (118 ml) butter, melted

¼ tsp kosher salt

1 cup (180 g) bittersweet chocolate chips

1 cup (180 g) milk chocolate chips

2 cups (473 ml) heavy cream

4 cups (200 g) mini marshmallows

2 cups (170 g) broken graham cracker pieces, approximately 7–8 sheets

¾ tsp smoked flaked salt, such as smoked Maldon

Preheat the oven to 350°F (177°C, or gas mark 4). Line a 9 x 13 x 2-inch (23 x 33 x 5-cm) baking pan with parchment paper or nonstick foil.

In a large bowl, mix together the graham cracker crumbs, melted butter and salt. Pour into the prepared pan and press evenly into the bottom. Bake for 15 to 20 minutes until the crust is lightly golden. Cool completely.

Place both bittersweet and milk chocolate chips in a large bowl. In a medium saucepan, bring the heavy cream to a boil. Remove the pan from the heat and pour the cream over the chocolate. Let the mixture sit for 5 minutes before whisking until smooth.

Add the mini marshmallows and graham cracker pieces, stirring well to ensure all the pieces are evenly coated with the chocolate ganache. Pour the mixture evenly over the cooled graham cracker crust. Sprinkle the top of the cookie bars with the smoked salt. Refrigerate for 1 to 2 hours until the filling is firm and set.

SALTED CARAMEL APPLE PIE

I have paired the iconic flavors of apples and caramel in this apple pie. Make sure you use a tart apple variety, such as Granny Smith, in this recipe as it complements the Salted Caramel Sauce (page 127). Don't undercook this pie. Make sure the crust is a deep golden brown before removing it from the oven for a crisp, buttery pie.

YIELD: 8 SERVINGS

2½ cups (312 g) all-purpose flour

1½ tbsp (18 g) sugar

1 tsp kosher salt

1 cup (230 g) cold butter, cut into ½-inch (1.5-cm) cubes

6–8 tbsp (90–120 ml) ice cold water

2 tsp (10 ml) apple cider vinegar

2 tbsp (30 ml) heavy cream

1 tbsp (12 g) raw sugar

¼ tsp flaked sea salt

FILLING

6 cups (1 kg) sliced, peeled Granny Smith apples

3 tbsp (28 g) cornstarch

1 cup (328 g) Salted Caramel Sauce (page 127)

Preheat the oven to 375°F (191°C, or gas mark 5).

Combine the flour, sugar and salt in the bowl of a food processor. Pulse 5 to 8 times to combine the dry ingredients. Add the cold butter, pulsing until the mixture resembles coarse crumbs. Add 6 tablespoons (90 ml) of water and the apple cider vinegar to the flour-butter mixture. Pulse until moist clumps form, add additional water 1 tablespoon (15 ml) at a time if the dough appears to be too dry. The mixture will not form a ball of dough.

Turn the dough onto a lightly floured surface and divide in half. Press each dough half into a disk, and wrap one half in plastic wrap and refrigerate. Roll out the first piece of dough on a lightly floured surface into a 13-inch (33-cm) round. Place into a 9½-inch (23-cm) pie dish and trim the excess dough leaving a ½-inch (1.5-cm) overhang.

To make the apple filling, toss together the sliced apples and cornstarch to evenly coat the apples. Add the salted caramel sauce and mix well.

Pour the apple filling into the pie crust. Remove the second piece of dough from the refrigerator and roll it out on a lightly floured surface into a 13-inch (33-cm) round. Gently place the dough on top of the pie, pressing the top and bottom edges of the pie crust together. Tuck the edge of the top pie crust under the edge of the bottom pie crust and crimp together in a decorative pattern with a fork or your fingers. Cut 6 vents in the top crust with a sharp knife.

Brush the entire top of the pie with the heavy cream, and sprinkle with raw sugar and flaked sea salt. Place the pie on a parchment-lined baking sheet. Bake for 55 to 65 minutes until the entire pie is a deep golden brown and the juices are bubbling out of the vents. Cool to room temperature before slicing.

SALTED CARAMEL PRETZEL BROWNIES

These fudgy brownies are swirled with Salted Caramel Sauce (page 127) and topped with bits of crunchy, salty pretzels. I gave a batch of these brownies to a friend who took them to work. She reported that her work was interrupted by the sound of her co-worker, a few offices down, moaning with pleasure as he bit into a brownie. So be warned that they are extremely addictive!

YIELD: 24 SQUARES

1 cup (230 g) butter

2 cups (360 g) bittersweet chocolate chips

1 cup (192 g) granulated sugar

1 cup (220 g) dark brown sugar, packed

2 tsp (10 ml) vanilla extract

5 large eggs

1 tsp kosher salt

1 cup plus 2 tbsp (141 g) all-purpose flour

¼ cup (28 g) unsweetened cocoa powder

½ cup (164 g) Salted Caramel Sauce (page 127)

½ cup (40 g) crushed pretzel twists

Preheat the oven to 350°F (177°C, or gas mark 4). Line a 9 x 13 x 2-inch (23 x 33 x 5-cm) baking pan with parchment paper or nonstick foil.

In a medium saucepan, melt the butter over medium-low heat, about 5 minutes, add the chocolate chips and remove from the heat. Let the chocolate sit in the warm butter for 3 to 5 minutes, and then mix together the chocolate and butter until smooth. Stir in the granulated sugar, brown sugar and vanilla.

Add the eggs, one at a time, mixing well after each addition. Add the salt, flour and cocoa powder. Mix until just combined. Pour the batter into the prepared pan.

Dollop spoonfuls of caramel sauce on top of the brownies and swirl into the batter using a knife. Sprinkle the top of the brownies with crushed pretzels. Bake for 25 to 30 minutes until a cake tester inserted into the middle comes out with a few moist crumbs. Cool completely before cutting into squares.

VANILLA SALT CANNELÉS

Cannelés are a small, French cake that has a dark, caramelized sugar exterior and a soft, custardy center. They are traditionally flavored with rum and vanilla. I finish my baked cannelés with a sprinkle of vanilla salt, and it provides a crunchy, salty contrast to the sweet exterior. Cannelés molds are needed for these cakes. Traditional molds are metal, but I like silicone ones, which can be easily found. The batter for these cakes also needs to rest in the refrigerator for at least 12 hours and up to 3 days, so be sure to plan ahead when making them.

YIELD: 16 CAKES

2 cups (473 ml) whole milk

1¼ cups (240 g) sugar

¼ tsp kosher salt

2 tbsp (29 g) butter

¼ cup (60 ml) dark rum

2 tsp (10 ml) vanilla extract

2 large eggs

2 egg yolks

1 cup (125 g) all-purpose flour

2 tbsp (29 g) butter, melted

½ tsp vanilla salt

Combine the milk, sugar, salt and butter in a small saucepan. Bring to a boil over medium heat, stirring to make sure the sugar dissolves, about 3 to 5 minutes. Remove from the heat, and add the rum and vanilla. Let cool for 10 minutes.

Place the eggs and egg yolks in a large bowl and whisk them together. Slowly add the warm milk in a steady stream, whisking constantly. Add the flour and whisk until well combined. Cover the bowl with plastic wrap, and refrigerate for at least 12 hours or up to 3 days.

When ready to bake the cannelés, brush the molds with the melted butter and place in the freezer for approximately 10 minutes to allow the butter to harden. Preheat the oven to 450°F (232°C, or gas mark 8).

Remove the batter from the refrigerator and whisk well, as the batter may have separated. Place the molds on a baking sheet and fill them ¾ full with batter. Bake for 30 minutes. Reduce the heat to 400°F (204°C, or gas mark 6) and bake for another 30 minutes.

The cannelés will become a very dark, mahogany brown color. Remove from the oven and allow to cool in the molds for 10 minutes. Remove the cannelés from the molds, and sprinkle the top of the still-warm cakes with a few flakes of vanilla salt. Allow to cool completely before serving.

SALTED CARAMEL CHOCOLATE TART WITH VANILLA SALT

My daughter Jemma hoards her favorite chocolate, caramel and shortbread candy bar every Halloween, and she absolutely forbids me from even taking a single bite. This tart is an ode to that candy bar—and when I make it, Jemma even allows me a few bites! The vanilla salt cuts through the buttery-sweetness of the caramel and the deep, rich chocolate. The sablé crust recipe makes enough dough for two tarts; use half the dough for this tart and use the other half to make the Grapefruit Tart (page 26).

YIELD: 8 TO 12 SERVINGS

½ cup plus 1 tbsp (130 g) butter, room temperature
½ cup (96 g) sugar
¼ tsp kosher salt
1 large egg
1¾ cups (219 g) all-purpose flour
¼ tsp vanilla salt

FILLING
1½ cups (492 g) Salted Caramel Sauce (page 127)
½ cup (118 ml) heavy cream
½ cup (90 g) bittersweet chocolate chips
1 tbsp (14 g) butter, room temperature

Preheat the oven to 350°F (177°C, or gas mark 4).

Cream together the butter, sugar and salt in the bowl of a stand mixer fitted with the paddle attachment. Add the egg and mix until blended. Add the flour and mix on low speed until just incorporated.

Divide the dough into 2 discs. Wrap 1 portion of dough in plastic wrap and save for future use. The dough can be refrigerated for up to a week or kept frozen for up to 1 month.

Roll the second portion of dough out on a lightly floured surface to an 11-inch (28-cm) round and gently fit into a 9-inch (23-cm) tart pan with removable bottom, pressing into the sides of tart pan. Trim the edges of the crust even with the top of the pan.

Refrigerate the tart shell for 30 minutes. Prick the bottom of the tart shell with the tines of a fork. Bake for 15 to 20 minutes until the entire shell is a light golden brown. Cool completely.

Pour the caramel sauce into the cooled tart shell and spread evenly. In a small saucepan, bring the heavy cream to a boil. Remove the pan from the heat. Add the chocolate and let the mixture sit for 5 minutes before whisking.

Add the butter, and whisk until completely combined and smooth. Pour the chocolate mixture over the caramel and gently spread evenly. Sprinkle the top of the tart with vanilla salt. Refrigerate for 30 minutes until the chocolate is set.

CHAPTER SEVEN

Basic Recipes, Tools and Ingredients

In this chapter, I share my can't-live-without basic recipes and my favorite ingredients. I also highlight tools that save time and make baking easier.

VANILLA ICE CREAM

This is my go-to ice cream recipe, and I love that it uses whole eggs and not just egg yolks. I use this as the base for many other ice cream variations by omitting the vanilla bean and adding other flavorings, whether it be different flavored liqueurs, fresh fruit, jams, candy pieces, broken cookies . . . The options are endless!

YIELD: APPROXIMATELY 2 PINTS (900 G)

2 cups (473 ml) heavy cream
1 cup (237 ml) whole milk
¾ cup (144 g) granulated sugar
¼ tsp kosher salt
1 large vanilla bean
2 large eggs

Combine the heavy cream, milk, sugar and salt in a medium saucepan. Split the vanilla bean. Scrape the seeds with a knife into the cream mixture and then add the scraped pods. Heat the mixture to just below a boil.

While the cream mixture is heating, whisk the eggs in a medium heatproof bowl. Add the hot cream in a steady stream to the eggs, whisking constantly. Pour the mixture back into the saucepan. Cook over medium-low heat, stirring constantly, until slightly thickened, about 5 to 7 minutes, and an instant-read thermometer reads 175°F (80°C).

Pour the custard through a fine-mesh sieve into a clean bowl. Cool to room temperature. Cover with plastic wrap and refrigerate until cold, at least 4 hours to overnight. Freeze in an ice cream maker according to manufacturer's instructions.

WHIPPED CREAM

There is ALWAYS a carton of heavy whipping cream in my fridge for use in baking, to pour in my coffee or to make fresh whipped cream to accompany any dessert. Nothing beats the flavor and billowy creaminess of fresh whipped cream. And it is easy to make!

YIELD: APPROXIMATELY 1½ CUPS (240 G)

1 cup (237 ml) heavy whipping cream
1 tbsp (8 g) powdered sugar

Place the cream and sugar in the bowl of a stand mixer fitted with the whisk attachment. Beat at medium-high speed for 4 to 6 minutes until soft peaks form.

INGREDIENTS

ALMOND PASTE

Almond paste is a mixture of ground almonds and sugar, and it can be found in both cans and tubes. Make sure not to use marzipan; it is a different product and will behave differently in the recipes.

BITTERS

Many years ago, I visited my sister in New York City and she took me to a shop that only sold bitters, salt and chocolate. I was in heaven and my obsession with bitters was born. The bitters that I use in this cookbook are angostura, orange, pumpkin or holiday, chocolate chili, cardamom and lavender. You can find most of these bitters in a good liquor store, or they can be found online. Definitely stock your pantry with these bitters as they really transform the flavors of my recipes.

BOURBON

My friends have nicknamed me "The Boozy Baker" because I use alcohol to flavor many of my desserts. Several recipes in this book call for bourbon. I haven't recommended any particular brand as I think it's important for you to choose your favorite.

BROWN SUGAR

Every recipe in this book that calls for brown sugar uses dark brown sugar. I prefer the deeper color and flavor that it has. Whenever measuring brown sugar, make sure it is packed in the measuring cup.

BUTTER

I love butter, and my fridge is often stocked with different types. I only use unsalted butter in my baking because I like to control the level of salt in a recipe. It is important to use the butter at the correct temperature, as stated in the recipes, for best results.

CITRIC ACID

I use food-grade citric acid in a few of the recipes in the Citrus chapter. Citric acid is a naturally occurring acid present in citrus fruits that contributes to their tart flavor. You can find food-grade citric acid online or from pharmacies. It is also the main ingredient in the containers of fresh fruit that you can buy at the grocery store.

CHOCOLATE

The quality of chocolate used in baking really affects the flavor and texture of desserts. I use good-quality milk and bittersweet chocolate chips in the recipes in this book. My go-to brand is the Belgian chocolate Callebaut, but use the chocolate that you enjoy eating!

COCKTAIL CHERRIES

I love either Luxardo maraschino cherries or amarena black cherries. Both come in a thick, flavorful cherry syrup that I also use in desserts and cocktails. A jar of either—or both—is definitely worth the splurge. They are a marked departure from the bright red cherries that come to mind when thinking about maraschino cherries.

COCOA POWDER

The only cocoa powder I use in my baking is unsweetened cocoa powder. Use a good-quality cocoa powder with a flavor that you like.

FINISHING SALTS

I am a confessed salt addict. At last count, I have over twenty varieties of finishing salts including black Hawaiian lava salt, truffle salt, lemon salt, coffee salt . . . The main salts I use in this cookbook are flaked sea salt, chili salt, smoked salt, lemon salt and vanilla salt. The brands I like the most for these salts are either Maldon or Jacobsen, and they are both available online. Once you've invested in these salts, they will keep indefinitely in your pantry, and you'll find yourself reaching for them for all of your cooking.

FLAVORED VINEGARS

There is an enormous selection of balsamic and flavored vinegars available in grocery and gourmet stores. I love using the different varieties in my baking or as a quick salad dressing. The main vinegars I use in the recipes in this book are a good-quality balsamic vinegar, unfiltered apple cider vinegar, blackberry balsamic vinegar, port vinegar, cherry balsamic vinegar and a white balsamic vinegar.

FLOURS

Almost all of my recipes in this book use all-purpose, white flour. I like using all-purpose flour in my baking so I don't have to keep multiple varieties of flour in my pantry. The Berry Crisp (page 111) uses both spelt and oat flours; they are naturally gluten-free and add a nice nuttiness to the recipe. You can find them in natural or health food stores in the bulk section, so you can buy just what you need for a recipe.

GRAHAM CRACKER CRUMBS

I keep a container of graham cracker crumbs in my pantry at all times. Buy pre-made graham cracker crumbs, or buy a few boxes of graham crackers and process them in a food processor to get a fine crumb. Store the crumbs in your panty in an airtight container; it saves a step when a recipe calls for graham cracker crumbs.

INSTANT ESPRESSO POWDER

For coffee flavor in my desserts, I like to use instant espresso powder as it provides a concentrated coffee flavor without adding extra water to a recipe.

KOSHER SALT

Other than the finishing salts that I use to sprinkle on top of a lot of my desserts, the only salt I use in the recipes in this book is kosher salt. The crystals are coarser than table salt, so don't use table salt in any of the recipes in this book or they will be much too salty.

LAVENDER

Dried culinary lavender is available in the spice section of many grocery stores. Or, if you are like me and have lavender bushes growing uncontrollably in your backyard, you can pick lavender and dry it for use in your baking.

LEMON JUICE POWDER

Lemon juice powder is concentrated lemon juice that is in a powdered form. I love using this ingredient to add a strong lemon juice flavor to a recipe without the added extra liquid of lemon juice. It is available from King Arthur Flour or from online retailers.

LEMON OIL

To achieve a strong, natural lemon flavor in many of my desserts I like to use pure lemon oil which is cold-pressed from lemon rinds. You can find it in many gourmet supermarkets or online. I used Boyajian brand lemon oil for the recipes in this book.

PUMPKIN

I have made my own pumpkin purée from scratch by roasting, cooling and puréeing a whole pumpkin, but I still prefer to use canned pumpkin purée. I like that the moisture content, color and flavor are always consistent. Make sure to use pure pumpkin purée and not a pumpkin pie mix that already contains spices and sugar.

ROSE WATER AND ORANGE BLOSSOM WATER

Flower waters are produced by the distillation of roses or orange blossoms. They are very concentrated and should be used sparingly. You want the flower essence in your baked goods; being heavy-handed with flower waters can cause a soapy flavor. Both rose water and orange blossom water can be found in ethnic grocery stores or in well-stocked liquor stores.

ROSE GERANIUM OIL

Rose geranium essential oil is the oil made from pressing rose geranium leaves. It has a floral fragrance and flavor. You can find edible essential oils at natural food and health food markets.

SPICES

I use a lot of different spices in my recipes that might not be present in your pantry. Many grocery stores sell small boxes of spices now, so you don't have to commit to an entire jar of the spice and you know that they will be fresh.

SWEETENED CONDENSED MILK

I always use full-fat sweetened condensed milk in my recipes. I don't like the texture of the low-fat variety.

VANILLA EXTRACT

Using a good-quality vanilla extract is a must when baking. I make my own vanilla extract in large quantities, and I love that my vanilla extract has specks of vanilla seeds in it. To make my vanilla extract, I scrape 10 vanilla beans, and I put both the pods and seeds in a very inexpensive 750-ml bottle of either vodka or bourbon. I let it steep for 2 to 4 weeks. As you use the vanilla extract, you can continue to top the bottle off with additional vodka or bourbon. I like to buy my vanilla beans from Beanilla.com.

YUZU JUICE

Yuzu is a citrus fruit that is native to Asia. It has a flavor that can be described as a mix of lemon, sour mandarin and grapefruit, and it has a floral scent. It can be found in bottles at well-stocked Asian grocery stores or from online retailers.

EQUIPMENT AND TOOLS

BAKING SHEETS

I easily have twenty baking sheets in my kitchen that are all the same size and nest together. I use them for everything from baking cookies to sorting LEGOs. I buy aluminum half sheet pans at restaurant supply stores that measure 18 x 13-inches (45 x 33-cm). They are sturdy, easy to wash and very reasonably priced.

CAKE TESTER

I received a cake tester in my Christmas stocking many years ago. It is a reusable metal skewer attached to a plastic handle and, at the time, I thought it was a frivolous kitchen tool. I have since been proven wrong. It has a home on the top of my oven, and I reach for it every time I need to check a cake, muffin or brownie. They are available online for a few dollars.

DEEP-DISH PIE PAN

All the recipes in this book that require a pie pan use a 9½-inch (24-cm) deep-dish glass pie pan. I like the capacity of the pan and the fact that I can see how the bottom crust is cooking. They are inexpensive so I can keep my kitchen stocked with a few of them.

FOOD PROCESSOR

I make all of my pie crust dough in the food processor. It quickly cuts the butter into the flour mixture without heating and melting the butter, and it consistently produces a super-flaky crust. A food processor is great for making cheesecake filling, as it blends the ingredients into a smooth mixture without incorporating too much air. It also makes quick work of chopping nuts and grinding cookies for crumbs.

IMMERSION BLENDER

I love my immersion blender and how easily and quickly it purées ingredients. It is my go-to piece of equipment when I have a small amount of food to purée so I don't have to get the blender out of the cupboard and clean it afterwards.

INSTANT-READ THERMOMETER

A good-quality, candy and oil thermometer is critical in baking to make sure the correct temperature is being reached in some recipes. I favor a digital thermometer that has an alarm that you can set to beep when the required temperature is reached. This alarm has saved me from having many burnt pans of sugar when making caramel sauce.

KITCHEN TORCH

You can buy kitchen torches from specialty kitchen stores that work great for caramelizing the sugar on top of a crème brûlée (page 39) or the pumpkin pie recipe (page 103) in this book. I had a smaller kitchen torch that I upgraded to a propane torch from the hardware store; I like the stronger flame it produces and it is also less expensive.

NONSTICK FOIL

I love using nonstick foil to line 9 x 13 x 2-inch (22 x 33 x 5-cm) pans. I also use it over parchment paper because you are able to mold it to fit perfectly in the pan. You can just lift your entire dessert right out of the pan for cutting and serving.

OVEN THERMOMETER

I think that the main reason for baking failures is using an oven that is set to the incorrect temperature. I have an oven thermometer in every oven I use, and I make sure to adjust the oven dials so that the oven temperature is accurate to the temperature stated in the recipe.

PARCHMENT PAPER

Almost every pan and baking tray that I use is lined with parchment paper before using. It provides a great nonstick surface and eases in the cleaning of the pans. I like to buy pre-cut sheets of parchment paper that perfectly fit my half sheet pans. It is available in bulk from restaurant supply stores.

SCOOPS

I have a variety of ice cream scoops that I use in my kitchen. They are definitely one of my critical tools as they allow equal portioning of batters and cookie dough. My favorite brand is Vollrath scoops; they are available in restaurant supply stores and online. I refer to the color of the handle for the scoop size in my recipes, which measure the following amounts:

Purple handled: ¾-ounce (22-g) or 4½ teaspoons

Black handled: 1-ounce (28-g) or 6 teaspoons

Red handled: 1⅓-ounce (38-g) or 8 teaspoons

Yellow handled: 1⅝-ounce (46-g) or 3¼ tablespoons

STAND MIXER

I received my first stand mixer as a birthday present over twenty years ago, and it is still the same mixer I used to develop all the recipes in this book. It is my workhorse and my lifesaver, and it is probably used on a daily basis. I use both the paddle and whisk attachments, and I have specified which one to use in every recipe.

ZESTER

A microplane zester is invaluable for zesting citrus fruit. It can also be used for grating fresh nutmeg or chocolate.

ACKNOWLEDGMENTS

It is completely surreal that I am writing acknowledgments at the end of my first cookbook. This journey has been an absolute joy. Seeing the culmination of my work and MY RECIPES in print is one of the proudest moments of my life.

To my little people, Jemma, Madeleine, Gavin and Nicky, who are my greatest and most honest taste testers. You never hesitated to tell me if you absolutely loved a recipe . . . or spat out a creation and told me that it was "just disgusting." This book is for you.

To my parents, Claude and Susan, and my sisters, Tasha and Miriam, who have always supported me and encouraged me and given me free rein of the kitchen despite my early aversion to cleaning up after myself. Thank you for allowing me to make your birthday cakes.

To Elizabeth and Gillas, for tirelessly eating, tasting, critiquing and taking home nearly every recipe in this book. For reading and editing and for encouraging me every step of the way.

To all my friends, for eating, buying, supporting, reading and enjoying my food and recipes. Your praise, love and belief in my talent have been invaluable. Thank you for celebrating this achievement with me.

To the team at Page Street Publishing, especially Elizabeth, who saw me on a TV show and took a chance on me to write my cookbook.

ABOUT THE AUTHOR

Jane Soudah is the pastry chef at Eveleigh Restaurant in West Hollywood, CA and the owner of an online bakery, Sweet Jane's Bakeshop. She won the 2016 *Spring Baking Championship* on Food Network. She was born in Seattle, grew up in London, England and she now lives with her four children (two sets of twins!) in Los Angeles, CA. Her background in Food Science and Safety helped her become the detail-oriented baker that she is today. When she isn't busy baking, creating new desserts and doing dessert research, Jane spends her time going on adventures with her kids, exploring Los Angeles with her friends and attending weekly whiskey tastings.

Jane has been in the kitchen and has had a love of baking since a young age. She obsessively reads food magazines, cookbooks and blogs, and she watches cooking shows on TV—all of which continue to provide instruction and inspiration.

Jane's recipes have been featured on Foodnetwork.com and in *Peloton*, *Cooking Light* and *People* magazines.

INDEX